RELIGION AND BEREAVEMENT

Counsel for the Physician — Advice for the Bereaved

Thoughts for the Clergyman

Edited by

Austin H. Kutscher
Lillian G. Kutscher
and

with 33 Contributing Clergymen
and 40 Contributing Clergymen Consultants

Health Sciences Publishing Corporation

New York, New York

1972

Library of Congress Cataloging in Publication Data

Kutscher, Austin H   comp.
  Religion and bereavement.

    1. Consolation—Addresses, essays, lectures. 2. Grief—Addresses,
essays, lectures. I. Kutscher, Lillian G., joint comp. II. Title.

BV4905.2.K86   242'.4   74-187977
ISBN 0-88238-515-1

Printed in the United States of America by
MEILEN PRESS INC., NEW YORK, N. Y.

TABLE OF CONTENTS

Table of Contents

D. *Coping with Grief*

PREFACE

From ministers of many faiths to the bereaved of many faiths come these messages of solace and words of reassurance for support in accepting inevitable facts in life and unchangeable events. There is at the *core* of every Western religion, whether or not the concept of immortality is espoused, an ineffable spiritual strength that can be transmitted by thoughts inspired by the tenets of a faith. What is so very striking is the fact that each man, while speaking from the altar of his own faith, can offer words of comfort that transcend the boundaries of parochial dogma or ritual.

This is an age of questioning: Is God dead? Of what use are traditional rituals? Should our faith rest in the answers offered by science? Is medical technology the salvation for a dying man's hopes? On whose conscience should rest the burden of selecting who will live and who will die? Should each individual be given the option of choosing the moment of his own death? Neither medical science nor medical ethics nor the agnostics, nor the atheist, nor the denigrator of religion have alternative or satisfying answers.

The hospital chaplain or the minister of each faith, from a base established by training and experiences which embrace failures and successes, can often be a source of counsel to the physician, effective advice for the bereaved, and productive thought to fellow clergymen. The dying and the bereaved and *all* their caregivers seek help from those who try to heal the body and those who try to ease the soul and mind. Linked together—each giving to and receiving from the other—the physician, his patient, the bereaved, and the clergy can and should reinforce the others' strengths with the courage of their own disciplines, their own beliefs, and their own consciences.

To disseminate further this interfaith exchange of views this collaborative book was written—for the physician charged with caring for the dying and the bereaved, the bereaved, and the clergyman called upon to heal the spirit and find a way to peaceful acceptance for those to whom he ministers.

A.H.K.

L.G.K.

CONTRIBUTORS

GENE E. BARTLETT, D.D., formerly *President*, Colgate-Rochester Divinity School, Rochester, New York

SANDRA BESS, West Hollywood, Florida, *Classical Literature*

IRWIN BLANK, D.D., *Rabbi*, Temple Sinai, Tenafly, New Jersey

DAVID R. BLUMENTHAL, *Rabbi*, Beth Emeth Synagogue, Larchmont, New York

GORDON K. BLUNT, *Minister*, Bethel Congregational Church, Ontario, California

Reverend WALTER DEBOLD, Englewood Cliffs College, Englewood, New Jersey

ROBERT A. EDGAR, M.A., D.D., *Minister*, Central Presbyterian Church, New York, New York

Reverend VINCENT PARIS FISH, *Vicar*, Church of the Holy Family, Lake Villa, Illinois

MARVIN GOLDFINE, *Jewish Chaplain*, The Presbyterian Hospital in the City of New York, Columbia-Presbyterian Medical Center, New York, New York (deceased)

Reverend GERALD C. HAMMON, *Minister*, First Christian Church, Selma, California

FREDERICK D. HAYES, D.D., *Minister*, High Street Congregational Church, Auburn, Maine

RICHARD C. HERTZ, D.D., *Rabbi*, Congregation Beth El, Detroit, Michigan

EDGAR N. JACKSON, D.D., *Former Pastor*, Mamaroneck Methodist Church, Mamaroneck, New York; *Chairman*, Advisory Board, Guidance Center of New Rochelle, New Rochelle, New York

WALTER JACOB, *Rabbi*, Temple Rodef Shalom, Pittsburgh, Pennsylvania

LeROY G. KERNEY, *Chaplain*, National Institutes of Health, Clinical Center, Bethesda, Maryland

AUSTIN H. KUTSCHER, D.D.S., *President*, Foundation of Thanatology; *Director*, Psychiatric Institute Dental Service, School of Dental and Oral Surgery, Columbia University. New York, New York

JOSEPH C. LANDRUD, Th.D., *Minister,* St. Paul's Lutheran Church, Monrovia, California; El Monte Counseling Service, El Monte, California

DAVID B. MAXWELL, *Associate Protestant Chaplain,* The Presbyterian Hospital in the City of New York, Columbia-Presbyterian Medical Center, New York, New York

WILLIAM B. McCULLOUGH, B.D., M.D., Department of Surgery, Yale Medical School, New Haven, Connecticut, *Member,* Presbytery of New York, The United Presbyterian Church in the U.S.A.

ROBERT L. MILES, M.D., *Private Practice,* Santa Barbara, California

GLENN R. MOSLEY, D.D., *Minister,* The Unity Center, Detroit, Michigan

SIDNEY NATHANSON, D.D., *Rabbi,* Temple Sholom, Plainfield, New Jersey

ROBERT PEEL, D.D., *Editorial Counselor,* Committee on Publication, The First Church of Christ Scientist, Boston, Massachusetts

NATHAN A. PERILMAN, D.D., *Rabbi,* Temple Emanuel, New York, New York

Reverend ROBERT B. REEVES, JR., *Chaplain,* The Presbyterian Hospital in the City of New York, Columbia-Presbyterian Medical Center, New York, New York

JAMES H. ROBINSON, D.D., *Director,* Operation Crossroads Africa, New York, New York

JACOB PHILIP RUDIN, D.D., *Rabbi,* Temple Beth-El, Great Neck, New York

ERVIN SEALE, D.D., *Minister,* Church of the Truth, New York, New York

DAVID J. SELIGSON, D.D., *Rabbi,* Central Synagogue, New York, New York

JACOB K. SHANKMAN, D.D., *Rabbi,* Temple Israel, New Rochelle, New York

PARK J. WHITE, M.D., *Director of the Department of Pediatrics,* Homer G. Phillips Hospital, St. Louis, Missouri; *Assistant Professor of Clinical Pediatrics (Emeritus),* Washington University School of Medicine, St. Louis, Missouri

CONTRIBUTING CONSULTANTS

RICHARD B. ADAMS, *Episcopalian Clergyman*, Bath, Maine

KRING ALLEN, *Disciples of Christ Clergyman*, Los Angeles, California

JACK AUSTIN, *Disciples of Christ Clergyman*, Peoria, Illinois

GEORGE RUSSELL BARBER, *Disciples of Christ Clergyman*, Los Angeles, California

GENE E. BARTLETT, D.D., *Protestant Clergyman*, Boston, Massachusetts, Contributor

GERHARD L. BELGUM, *Lutheran Clergyman*, Lakewood, California

GORDON K. BLUNT, *United Church of Christ Clergyman*, Ontario, California, Contributor

GERALD BOYLE, *Catholic Clergyman*, Goshen, New York

CARL B. CAMP, *Baptist Clergyman*, Glenview, Illinois

ARNE CHRISTIANSON, *Lutheran Clergyman*, San Diego, California

ROBERT C. CLARK, *Disciples of Christ Clergyman*, Blue Mound, Illinois

AUSTIN COE, *Disciples of Christ Clergyman*, Downey, California

JOHN L. COLBURN, *United Church of Christ Clergyman*, Los Angeles, California

GILBERT DANIEL, *Pastor*, Cameron, Illinois

GEORGE A. DETOR, *Episcopalian Clergyman*, Buena Park, California

JOEL DUFFIELD, *Pastor*, Hamilton, Illinois

CHARLES DUNCAN, *Baptist Clergyman*, Joliet, Illinois

ROBERT A. EDGAR, M.A., D.D., *Presbyterian Clergyman*, New York, New York, Contributor

VINCENT PARIS FISH, *Episcopalian Clergyman*, Lake Villa, Illinois, Contributor

MARVIN GOLDFINE, *Rabbi*, New York, New York, Contributor (deceased)

WILLIAM GUTKNECHT JR., *Lutheran Clergyman*, Lodi, California

GERALD C. HAMMON, *Disciples of Christ Clergyman*, Winters, California

F. D. HAYES, D.D. *United Church of Christ Clergyman*, Auburn, Maine, Contributor

RICHARD C. HERTZ, D.D., *Rabbi*, Detroit, Michigan, Contributor

E. HOLLAND, *Lutheran Clergyman*, Fremont, California

WALLACE O. KLANDRUD, *Lutheran Clergyman*, Camarillo, California

JOSEPH C. LANDRUD, Th.D. *Lutheran Clergyman*, Monrovia, California, Contributor

EDWARD LARAMIE, *Catholic Clergyman*, Arlington Heights, Illinois

H. FREDERICK MORE, *Lutheran Clergyman*, Augusta, Maine

HENREY MOSER, *Baptist Clergyman*, Granite City, Illinois

SIDNEY NATHANSON, D.D., *Rabbi*, Plainfield, New Jersey, Contributor

JAMES O'REILLY, *Catholic Clergyman*, Birmingham, Alabama

JOHN ORPEN, *Episcopalian Clergyman*, Chicago, Illinois

NATHAN A. PERILMAN, D.D. *Rabbi*, New York, New York, Contributor

CHARLES H. PERRY, *Episcopalian Clergyman*, Sacramento, California

ROBERT B. REEVES, JR., *Protestant Clergyman*, New York, New York, Contributor

GEOFFREY SELTH, *Unitarian Clergyman*, Santa Rosa, California

JOHN TUMELTY, *Catholic Clergyman*, Alexander City, Alabama

ANTHONY ZOGHBY, *Catholic Clergyman*, Prichard, Alabama

Anonymous Catholic Clergyman, Rural New York State

INDEX OF AUTHORS
(In Chronological Order)

Rabbi Meir: Second Century A.D. Palestinian teacher.

St. Augustine: 354-430: Doctor of the Church, one of the four Latin fathers, and bishop of Hippo, North Africa. His influence on Christianity is thought to be second only to St. Paul, and theologians—Roman Catholic and Protestant—look upon him as the founder of theology.

John Donne: 1572-1631: English poet and divine. He was made Dean of St. Paul's Cathedral in 1621. His poems and sermons have had great influence on modern English poetry.

*Ralph Waldo Emerson: 1803-1882: American writer, philosopher and ex-Unitarian minister. In his transcendental philosophy, outward phenomenon are viewed as symbols of man's inner life. His poems and essays profoundly influenced American thought of the nineteenth century—and continue to do so even today.

Cardinal Henry Edward Manning: 1808-1892: English churchman and Cardinal of the Roman Church in 1875. A zealous pastor, he greatly expanded Catholic education in England and furthered the education of the poor.

---

* Note: Biographical material obtained from the *Columbia Encyclopedia* and the *Concise Dictionary of Literature*.

A. UNDERSTANDING GRIEF

THE IMPORTANCE OF UNDERSTANDING GRIEF

Edgar N. Jackson

It is important for us to know what grief is and how it works, for we have discovered that it is a major source of illness and distress to body, mind and spirit. Research in psychosomatic medicine indicates that certain forms of illness are actually ways by which the organism acts out its grief. Admissions to general hospitals are more numerous among the grief-stricken than among the general population; an examination of admissions to hospitals for the mentally and emotionally ill clearly indicates that many depressions are related to grief. Often spiritual crises develop with the loss of meaning for life and acute despair that comes with grief, and the percentage of suicides and suicide attempts among the grieving is above average.

One of the problems in understanding grief is that it is often camouflaged. In some it may appear as a subtle change of character. In others it may take the form of increased dependence on sedation, tranquilizers or alcohol. In yet others it may be acted out in aggression, hostility or exaggerated independence. Each person is unique and brings into every new experience his own individual and varied responses.

The problem of coping with grief in our culture is also somewhat different from that of the past. Grief is an experience of acute deprivation. In an affluent society there is less experience in adjusting to deprivation and so there is less preparation for the injured personality to manage the new and disrupting experience of death.

Our culture is not only affluent but also death-denying and death-defying. Such denial limits both the opportunity to talk out and act out deep feelings of grief. It tends to isolate and leave the grief-stricken emotionally unsupported. Thus, the bereaved's spontaneous expressions of grief are rejected and made to appear inappropriate. Even the social devices which support the expression of emotion (e.g., those within our religious institutions) are being modified to conform to the death-defying mood and so the bereaved person is doubly denied at the time when his need is most acute. The importance of acting out deep feelings through rites, rituals and ceremonials has special

3

value when dealing with the emotions that are too intense to be put into words.

Responses to grief are often misinterpreted because there appears to be no direct relationship between them and their cause. For example, some bereaved attempt to manage the emotional capital they are obliged to withdraw from the lost love object by immediately and unwisely reinvesting it. Or they establish strong relationships to physicians, pastors, or others involved with them in the emotional crisis.

Invariably accompanying grief there is guilt—real, neurotic or existential. This grows from the ambivalent nature of love itself, with its contrasts of responsibility and privilege, sorrow and joy, benefits and deprivations. When death comes, life is reconsidered, and the bereaved tends to think of what might have been had he acted differently. Some persons are overwhelmed by feelings of guilt and try to punish themselves by self-injury, self-deprivation or self-rejection.

Some of the funeral rituals provide ways in which people can begin to work through their guilt feelings. Sometimes this is done by the final gift provided for the deceased (the casket and/or floral decorations), by gifts to the bereaved or the dedication of a memorial. Giftgiving, generally employed as a device for acting out guilt feelings, is a symbolic form of retribution when real retribution is no longer possible because of the death.

It should be noted that the person in grief needs a philosophical base which affirms the value of life. The rites and ceremonials at the time of death serve to verify these ideas for the grieving individual and for the supporting community which needs to re-assert its viability.

This philosophical basis would necessarily include: a concept of purpose that is adequate to give a significant meaning to his life and the lives of others; a concept of man as a being with sustaining spiritual value; a concept of God as essential goodness; a concept of historical continuity and a concept of an undying quality of some portion of what he may call his own soul. Such a philosophy would be an achievement of the individual and would bear the marks of his own need and the qualities of his own personality. These would be the elements of the faith he would live by. It is often the fact of death that stimulates one to formulate some such conceptualization.

Sometimes the bereaved is so disturbed by the emotion and physical reactions that possess him that he feels he is becoming emotionally disorganized. It is important to realize that grief has the characteristics of a neurosis, and the bereaved may well show such symptoms and suffer feelings out of the ordinary. Physically, these symptoms may include shortness of breath, a choking sensation, sighing and crying, sometimes to hysterical proportions. Symptoms may also include nausea, loss of appetite, loss of sphincter controls or compulsive eating and drinking, weakness of the large muscle system, dizziness, faintness and an overall feeling of distress. All are quite normal and nothing to be alarmed about if they do not persist over a lengthy period.

These expressions of grief can be considered pathological when they are prolonged over extended periods of time or when they do not appear at all. The person who shows no feeling may be in more difficulty than the one who does. We do not choose whether or not we have feelings, but only how they will be managed. When feelings are so powerful that they cannot be coped with they are apt to be repressed, denied or detoured—in the form of psychosomatic illness, through the development of inappropriate responses to similar situations which threaten loss, or in disruption of his basic value structure.

The seriously disturbed person who is not able to function normally in meeting his own needs or in his basic relationships with others should have the benefits of treatment from those who are professionally qualified.

Grief work is the natural process by which the emotions reorganize themselves to cope with the loss and to reestablish healthful relationships. The essential processes of grief work are: first, the facing of the physical reality with all of its implications; second, the recognition and expression of the emotions that are relevant to the physical event; third, working through of the emotions by talking them out in visitations and family events or with trusted counselors, and also by acting out the deep feelings through appropriate rites, rituals, and ceremonials; fourth, the acceptance of emotional support from the general community, the religious or spiritual community and the supportive family. The grief-stricken are probably more dependent emotionally than they have been at any time since their early childhood. To deny this may create emotional hazards. To accept the facts and the feelings as well as the emotional support provided may be a major resource in hastening the process of wise grief management.

Grief work is painful and the bereaved may seek relief in drugs. This usually does not serve a therapeutic purpose, but only postpones to a less appropriate time and place the feelings with which he must deal. Unless there is a special medical problem it is usually best to face the painful facts that confirm the reality of the event. Perhaps one of the soundest of procedures for resolving psychological denial is the traditional practice of "viewing the remains." This often produces a breakthrough of denied feelings and hastens the grief work.

Grief work is usually accomplished through the normal resources provided by church and community, but increasingly these are being curtailed by a death-denying, death-defying culture, so it may be necessary to develop compensating resources for both individual and community. This means increased counseling services and a more imaginative use of traditional practices.

Man is mortal and his life will end. Denial of this can be philosophically and personally devastating. The ability to live life creatively with an awareness of the mortal limits of existence is essential to true maturity. The ability to face death may be one of the resources needed to build a realistic and competent philosophical base for living.

Understanding grief as a profound emotion, the other side of the coin of love, gives one a sounder base for interpreting the meaning of life itself. This understanding gives a structure of values for living, and the resources for a kind of courage that does not fear life because it recognizes that life must be lived within mortal bounds. A wise reexamination and an imaginative development of resources may make it possible for us to understand and manage the powerful emotions of grief so that life may grow through these emotions rather than be destroyed by them.

DEATH IN CHRIST

Walter Debold

We want you to be quite certain, brothers, about those who have died, to make sure that you do not grieve about them, like the other people who have no hope. We believe that Jesus died and rose again, and that it will be the same for those who have died in Jesus: God will bring them with him. We can tell you this from the Lord's own teaching, that any of us who are left alive until the Lord's coming will not have any advantage over those who have died. At the trumpet of God, the voice of the archangel will call out the command and the Lord himself will come down from heaven; those who have died in Christ will be the first to rise, and then those of us who are still alive will be taken up, in the clouds, together with them, to meet the Lord in the air. So we shall stay with the Lord forever. With such thoughts as these you should comfort one another.[1]

For Catholics, there are several texts that are capable of instructing and, simultaneously, consoling those who mourn. The mass on the day of burial incorporates two readings. The above, from Paul's first letter to the Thessalonians, offers comfort by the promise of resurrection.

The second reading, from the Gospel according to John, offers comfort by recounting the dialogue between Jesus and the grieving sister of the dead Lazarus. Christ presents himself as the one on whom the Christian hope for eternal life is based: he uses a mystery-filled expression, "I am the resurrection."

Martha said to Jesus, "If you had been here, my brother would not have died, but I know that, even now, whatever you ask of God, he will grant you." "Your brother," said Jesus to her, "will rise again." Martha said, "I know he will rise again at the resurrection on the last day." Jesus said, "I am the resurrection. If anyone believes in me, even though he dies he will live, and whoever lives and believes in me will never die. Do you believe

---

1. 1 Thessalonians 4, 13-18.

this?" "Yes, Lord," she said, "I believe that you are the Christ, the Son of God, the one who was to come into this world." [2]

Other masses for the deceased employ a variety of scriptural passages to console those who mourn.

> When this perishable nature has put on imperishability, and when this mortal nature has put on immortality, then the words of scripture will come true: "Death is swallowed up in victory. Death, where is your victory? Death, where is your sting?[3]
>
> I tell you most solemnly, the hour will come—in fact it is here already—when the dead will hear the voice of the Son of God, and all who hear it will live. For the Father, who is the source of life, has made the Son the source of life . . .[4]
>
> Happy are those who die in the Lord! Happy indeed, the Spirit says; now they can rest for ever after their work, since their good deeds go with them.[5]
>
> I am the living bread which has come down from heaven. Anyone who eats this bread will live forever." [6]

Other passages in the Christian scriptures are calculated to console one in the face of death. Some hint at, and others plainly promise, a deathless life to come. But what is the nature of this life-after-death? In faith, can we look forward to reunion? On what can I base this hope?

When pressed on this point, Jesus gave answers that were rather those of the poet or mystic than of the philosopher. One time he said, in a way that was warm but laconic: "there are many rooms in my Father's house." [7] He seems to imply that there are not many things in human experience that can help to comprehend the infinite Truth, Goodness and Beauty awaiting us in the Land of Promise. In fact, it is expressly said by Paul: " . . . no eye has seen and no ear has

---

2. John 11, 21-27.
3. 1 Corinthians 15, 54-55.
4. John 5, 25-26.
5. Apocalypse 14, 13.
6. John 6, 51.
7. John 14, 2.

heard, things beyond the mind of man, all that God has prepared for those who love him." [8]

The Song of Songs can be read as a promise that earthly love will prove to have been a foretaste of the eternal.

Yet how am I to adjust now to the present? Am I to be philosophical? The Creator has placed us on this planet and faced us toward the future. Located in history, the human person must look to horizons, to goals. But more, he must pursue these goals; to fulfill his humanity he must advance toward the horizon. With the companionship of loved ones this is possible. Deprived of that companionship, the journey seems pointless and endless.

One does not ordinarily attempt to console with the language of the theologian or the philosopher. Nevertheless, their perceptions, their distinctions and methodical formulations can prepare us ahead of time for the tragic events that make us question, "Why?" The love that gave life meaning is gone. Taken away. By whom is it taken? By God? But if God acts so absurdly, is not life itself absurd? What kind of God is this who gives and takes away?

The Christian theologian acknowledges the tragic element in death. He sees it in this light as a "death of Adam." But, in the light of his faith, he recognizes it as something that is capable of being transfigured: It can be a "death in Christ."

Death as merely "human," as the end of existence for one individual member of sinful mankind, symbolizes man's alienation from God. But, since a Redeemer has come, even this aspect of man's experience is redeemed. The believer whose life has been oriented toward the divine will is a person whose death is Christ-like in its intention: his will is to surrender himself into the hands of God. He would, therefore, find life by losing it: "Father, into your hands I commit my spirit." [9]

At the graveside the bereaved recite what is sometimes called a New Testament psalm referred to as the "Benedictus" from its first

---

8. 1 Corinthians 2, 9.
9. Luke 23, 46.

word in the Latin version: "Blessed be the Lord, the God of Israel, for he has visited his people. . . ." [10] According to St. Luke, these words were the first utterance of Zechariah, the father of John the Baptist, on the occasion of the circumcision of his son. The prayer contains the elements of praise, remembrance and thanksgiving that are characteristic of the Judaic tradition. In the Christian ritual it has many applications, but it is invariably a prayer of "beginnings." As such, its inclusion in the burial rite is significant: It implies that this death is not so much an end as a beginning. One verse, echoing Isaiah 9, 1, speaks of "our God who from on high will bring the rising Sun to visit us, to give light to those who live in darkness and the shadow of death, and to guide our feet into the way of peace." [11]

Indeed, then, death is the end of an earthly pilgrimage, but it is also the fulfillment of existence. Its mystery is profound. Since the Savior experienced all of man's humanness, even undergoing death he altered the meaning of our existence—even of its termination in time. No longer is dying merely a symbol of alienation from the Father, nor merely a necessary evil which demonstrates our oneness with Adam in the community of sin. Now it is sacramentalized. It is a holy thing. Dying "in Christ" is a means of union with the "new Adam." It is a way of participating in his new life; it is an unfolding to full maturity. Purified of egoism, the fully developed person, with freedom unrestrained, is able to be face to face with him who is able to say, "Let there be lights . . ." [12]

The mystery that is the life-death-resurrection of Jesus is that central reality in which the whole life of the Christian is caught up. One's existence is grounded in Christ in Baptism: "You have been buried with him when you were baptised; and by baptism, too, you have been raised up with him through your belief in the power of God who raised him from the dead." [13] This initiation into the mystery was completed and continually renewed throughout life by the celebration of the Eucharist. This colors life with joyful expectancy: From the earliest days a most characteristic Christian prayer,

---

10. Luke 1, 68.
11. Luke 1, 79.
12. Genesis 1, 14.
13. Colossians 2, 12.

"Maran Atha," [14] reflects this eager anticipation. In translation, these Aramaic words mean "The Lord is coming," or "Lord, come!"

The book of Job is one part of the Bible that considers the problem of evil in its totality. As one begins the book, evil is seen to have the nature of mystery; the mystery is probed, but it is still there at the end. In the 38th chapter God says to Job, in effect, "Who are you to ask for justifications?" Indeed, he says, "Where were you when I laid the earth's foundation?"[15] "Have you ever in your life given orders to the morning or sent the dawn to its post . . ." [16] This sort of interrogation does not dishearten Job. In spite of all his sufferings, he will never cease to give praise to the Almighty one. Even if the problem of evil is beyond solution, never will this faithful man cease to proclaim, "Blessed be the name of Yahweh!" [17] The nearest he can come to a solution in human terms is in the acknowledgment that God "brings all men's strivings to a standstill so that each must acknowledge his hand at work." [18] Job is the man of faith whose love of God is equal to the challenge that mystery poses. For him, "love is strong as Death." [19]

The Christian Message has been proclaimed. What effect does it have upon the way that men approach their last moments? For an answer let us look to the last days of three members of the Church. These three are alike in that they faced their end with full awareness and great courage. From every other point of view they are diverse.

The first of these three is Joan of Arc. On May 30, 1431, she was burned at the stake in Rouen after a five-month trial for heresy. That day her ashes were thrown into the Seine. Five hundred years later it is still customary, on the anniversay of her death, for girls dressed in white to assemble on that spot and cast white flowers upon the same river.[20] They keep alive the memory of the Maid, for they know

---

14. 1 Corinthians 16, 22.
15. Job 38, 4.
16. Job 38, 12.
17. Job 1, 21.
18. Job 37, 7.
19. Song of Songs 8, 6.
20. Sven Stolpe, *The Maid of Orleans*. New York, Pantheon, 1956, p. 286.

how she died. During her trial Joan testified, "I will maintain what I have said until death." [21] At seven o'clock on the morning of May 30, a confessor absolved her and gave her the Eucharist. "Where shall I be tonight?" she asked him. He replied, "Have you no faith in our Lord?" "Yes," she replied, "God helping me, today I shall be with Him in paradise." [22]

As her body burned, a crucifix was held up before her eyes. Her last words were, "Jesus! Jesus!"

A century later, Sir Thomas More, Lord Chancellor of England, was beheaded after fourteen months imprisonment in the Tower of London. From his prison cell, two months before he was executed, Thomas wrote to his daughter:

> I do nobody harm, I say no harm, I think no harm, but wish everybody good. And if this be not enough to keep a man alive, in good faith I long not to live. And I am dying already, and have, since I came here, been diverse times in the condition where I thought to die within one hour. And I thank our Lord that I was never sorry for it, but rather sorry when I saw the pang past. And therefore my poor body is at the King's pleasure. Would God my death might do him good![23]

In the script for *A Man for All Seasons,* Thomas Bolt preserved the memory of More's courage to the last. He had him say to the executioner on the scaffold: "Friend, be not afraid of your office. You send me to God." [24]

We of the twentieth century remember well Pope John XXIII. He had come to the papacy in his old age but, with enthusiasm and great vigor, he initiated the history-making ecumenical council known as Vatican II. Several times he expressed doubts that he would live to

---

21. *The Trial of Joan of Arc,* translated by W. S. Scott, Westport, Connecticut, Associated Booksellers, 1956, p. 162.

22. *Ibid.,* p. 171.

23. *The Utopia of Sir Thomas More,* modernized text by Mildred Campbell. New York, Walter J. Black, 1947, p. 302.

24. Robert Bolt, *A Man for All Seasons.* New York, Random House, 1962, p. 162.

see the council brought to completion. Nor did he. Pope John approached death with full awareness. In 1961, at the age of eighty, he wrote in his diary: "As always, I desire nothing more or less than what the Lord continues to give me. I thank and bless Him every day, and I am ready for anything." [25] On June 3, 1963, he went to his reward.

Ideally, every Christian should be able to say with Paul, "Life to me, of course, is Christ, but then death would bring me something more . . ." [26] What more? Job gives an answer to that:

> This I know: that my Avenger lives, and he, the Last, will take his stand on earth. After my awaking, he will set me close to him, and from my flesh I shall look on God.[27]

---

25. Pope John XXIII, *Journal of a Soul,* translated by Dorothy White. New York, McGraw-Hill Book Company, 1964, p. 319.

26. Philipians 1, 21.

27. Job 19, 25-26.
   The Scripture citations are from *The Jerusalem Bible.*
   New York, Doubleday and Company, 1966.

THRENODIES OF THEOLOGY

SANDRA BESS

"God of our Fathers, what is man!"
(Milton, *Samson Agonistes*)

Indeed, what is man who seeks freedom in life, life in death, and the death of all death? What is man who cries to his God, "Behold, I cry out of wrong, but I am not heard . . ."[1] ". . . behold me, how unjust are my sufferings."[2] Philosopher, poet and priest have stormed the boundaries of earth and heaven, have searched the depths of their souls and their hearts to give man an answer to *what* is Man, *who* is Man, and *why* is Death. Each of us seeks answers in a time of great travail, particularly upon the loss of a loved one. Each of us becomes then in his grieving "moments" of loss and within his own despairing soul, a philosopher, striving for answers through reason; a poet, seeking answers beyond reason; and a priest, solemnizing answers through faith. These three inner voices help define the terms of one's sorrow, intertwined as they are during a time of grief with the tragic vision of life.

Whether or not the bereaved believes that his loved one has been returned to dust, endowed with a dreamless sleep, suspended in the void of nothingness, or transported to the Kingdom of God, Death remains the great equalizer of humanity and Sorrow her handmaiden. Philosophy, Poetry and Religion, the trinity of life and the godhead of the soul, are the children of Death . . . and the guardians of man's eternal love.

The works contained herein are concerned with these same personal inner voices of a handful of preeminent clergymen who, by nature and spiritual disposition, were also gifted poets and philosophers. These men, devoted to the service of God, knew the devastating power of death. In seeking to assuage their own grief and the grief of others, they illuminated their struggle by their faith in the existence of God, His justice and His love. Their faith in God, con-

---

1. *The Book of Job.*
2. Aeschylus, *Prometheus.*

stantly challenged and laboriously realized, evokes a vision of an eternal world where love is stronger than death, where sorrow is the spiritual component of joy, and darkness, the genesis of light. In these excerpts, spanning eighteen centuries of theological writings, are contained many philosophical truths and poetic imaginings, as well as religious beliefs. For in man's time of sorrow, he seeks the rhyme and riddle of life to give truth, beauty and faith a meaning beyond mortality. The stoic voice of the philosopher within man proclaims truth: "What is mine shall forever be mine . . ." The eloquent song of the poet sings of beauty: "What is mine shall be born anew . . ." The fervent prayer of the priest extols holiness: "What is mine is God's . . ." This is indeed the trinity of life and the godhead of the soul!

from THE CONFESSIONS OF ST. AUGUSTINE

The Death of A Friend

My heart was made dark by sorrow, and whatever I looked upon was death. My native place was a torment to me, and my father's house was a strange unhappiness. Whatsoever I had done together with him was, apart from him, turned into a cruel torture. My eyes sought for him on every side, and he was not given to them. I hated all things, because they no longer held him. Nor could they now say to me, "Here he comes," as they did in his absence from them when he lived. To myself I became a great riddle, and I questioned my soul as to why it was sad and why it afflicted me so grievously, and it could answer me nothing. If I said to it, "Hope in God," it did right not to obey me, for the man, that most dear one whom she had lost, was more real and more good to her than the fantasy in which she was bade to hope. Only weeping was sweet to me, and it succeeded to my friend in my soul's delights.

A Sweet Sorrow

Lord, these things have now passed away and time has eased my wound. Am I able to hearken to you, who are truth, and to turn my heart's ear to your mouth, that you may tell me why weeping is sweet to those in misery? Is it that you, although present in all places, have flung our misery far away from yourself, and do you abide unchanged in yourself, while we are spun about in our trials? Yet unless we could weep into your ears, no trace of hope would remain for us. Whence is it, then, that sweet fruit is plucked from life's bitterness, from mourning and weeping, from sighing and lamenting? Does sweetness lie there because we hope that you will graciously hear us? This rightly holds for our prayers, since they contain our desire of attaining to you. But does it hold for that grief and mourning over what was lost, with which I was overwhelmed? I did not hope that he would come back to life, nor did I beg for that by my tears; I only sorrowed and wept, for I was wretched and I had lost my joy. Or is weeping itself a bitter thing, and does it give us pleasure because of distaste for things in which we once took joy, but only at such times as we shrink back from them?

His Love for the Lost Friend

Why do I speak of these things? For now is not the time for questioning, but for confessing to you. Wretched was I, and wretched is every soul that is bound fast by friendship for mortal things, that is torn asunder when it loses them, and then first feels the misery by which it is wretched even before it loses those things. Such was I at that time, and I wept most bitterly and I found rest in my bitterness. So wretched was I that I held that life of wretchedness to be more dear to me than my friend himself. For although I wished to change it, yet I was more unwilling to lose it than I was to lose my friend . . . for most heavily there weighed upon me both weariness of life and fear of dying. I believe that the more I loved him, the more did I hate and fear death, which had taken him away from me, as my cruelest enemy. I thought that it would speedily devour all men, since it had been able to devour him. All this I was, and I remember it.

Behold my heart, my God, behold what is within it! See this, for I remember it, O you who are my hope, who cleanse me from the uncleanness of such affections, who direct my eyes to you and pluck my feet out of the snare. I marveled that other men should live, because he, whom I had loved as if he would never die, was dead. I marveled more that I, his second self, could live when he was dead. Well has someone said of his friend that he is half of his soul. For I

17

thought that my soul and his soul were but one soul in two bodies. Therefore, my life was a horror to me, because I would not live as but a half. Perhaps because of this I feared to die, lest he whom I had loved so much should wholly die.

Departure from Thagaste

O madness, which does not know how to love men, as men should be loved! O foolish man, who so rebelliously endures man's lot! Such was I at that time. Therefore I raged, and sighed, and wept, and became distraught, and there was for me neither rest nor reason. I carried about my pierced and bloodied soul, rebellious at being carried by me, but I could find no place where I might put it down. Not in pleasant groves, not in games and singing, not in sweet-scented spots, not in rich banquets, not in the pleasure of the bedchamber, not even in books and in poetry did it find rest. All things grew loathsome, even the very light itself; and whatsoever was not he was base and wearisome to me—all except groans and tears, for in them alone was found a little rest. But when my soul was withdrawn from these, a mighty burden of misery weighed me down. To you, O lord, ought it to have been lifted up, to be eased by you. I knew it, but I willed it not, nor was I able to will it, and this the more because for me, when I thought upon you, you were not something solid and firm. For to me then you were not what you are, but an empty phantom, and my error was my god. If I attempted to put my burden there, so that it might rest, it hurtled back upon me through the void, and I myself remained an unhappy place where I could not abide and from which I could depart. For where could my heart fly to, away from my heart? Where could I fly to, apart from my own self? Where would I not pursue myself? But still I fled from my native town. Less often would my eyes seek him where they were not used to seeing him, and from Thagaste I came to Carthage.

The Healing Powers of Time and Change

Time does not take time off, nor does it turn without purpose through our senses: it works wondrous effects in our minds. See how it came and went from day to day, and by coming and going it planted in me other hopes and other memories, and little by little they filled me up again with my former sources of delight. My sorrow gave way to them, but to it succeeded not new sorrows, but yet causes of new sorrows. Why did that sorrow penetrate so easily into my deepest being, unless because I had poured out my soul upon the sand by loving a man soon to die as though he were one who would never die? Most of all, the solace of other friends restored and revived me, and together with them I loved what I loved in place of you.

. . . There were other things done in their company which more completely seized my mind: to talk and to laugh with them; to do friendly acts of service for one another; to read well-written books together; sometimes to tell jokes and sometimes to be serious; to disagree at times, but without hard feelings, just as a man does with himself; and to keep our many discussions pleasant by the very rarity of such differences; to teach things to the others and to learn from them; to long impatiently for those who were absent, and to receive with joy those joining us. These and similar expressions, proceeding from the hearts of those who loved and repaid their comrades' love, by way of countenance, tongue, eyes, and a thousand pleasing gestures, were like fuel to set our minds ablaze and to make but one out of many.

St. Augustine

THE MOURNING OF RABBI MEIR

As Rabbi Meir sat in the *Beth Ha-Medrish* (school) one Sabbath day, toward the hour of Minchah (the afternoon prayer), his two children died at home. His wife put them both in one bed and covered them. When the Sabbath was ended Rabbi Meir returned to his home, and asked: "Where are the children?" "They went to the *Beth Ha-Medrish*," answered his wife. "I waited for them and I did not see them," said Rabbi Meir. Then his wife gave him the bowl of wine, he made the Havdalah (farewell prayer to the Sabbath) and asked again: "Where are the children?" And she answered: "They have gone out and will return." She then served the meal, and when he had eaten he made the benediction. When he was done his wife said: "Rabbi, I have a question to ask." "Speak." "Rabbi, a man was here some time ago and left a sum of money with me. He is

19

coming now to claim it. Shall I return it to him or not?" "My child, whosoever has something in trust for another, must return it to the owner." "I did not want to return it without your knowledge of it." And then she took Rabbi Meir by the hand, brought him into the room and over to the bed, and drew back the cover that lay on her children; and he saw them lying dead on the bed. And he cried out: "My children, my children, my teachers, my teachers! My children who reverenced me, my teachers who enlightened me!" Then his wife said: "Did you not say that what I held in trust I must return to the Owner?" And he replied: "The Lord giveth, the Lord taketh away, blessed be the name of the Lord."

Rabbi Meir

EXCERPTS

We never have more than we can bear. The present hour we are always able to endure. As our day, so is our strength. If the trials of many years were gathered into one, they would overwhelm us; therefore, in pity to our little strength, He sends first one, then another, then removes both, and lays on a third, heavier, perhaps, than either; but all is so wisely measured to our strength that the bruised reed is never broken. We do not enough look at our trials in this continuous and successive view. Each one is sent to teach us something, and altogether they have a lesson which is beyond the power of any to teach alone.

o   o   o   o   o

Let us learn from this communion of saints to live in hope. Those who are now at rest were once like ourselves. They were once weak, faulty, sinful; they had their burdens and hindrances, their slumbering and weariness, their failures and their falls. But now they have overcome. Their life was once homely and commonplace. Their day ran out as ours. Morning and noon and night came and went to them as to us. Their life, too, was as lonely and sad as yours. Little fretful circumstances and frequent disturbing changes wasted away their hours as yours. There is nothing in your life that was not in theirs; there was nothing in theirs but may be also in your own. They have overcome, each one, and one by one; each in his turn, when the day came, and God called him to the trial. And so shall you likewise.

✿   ✿   ✿   ✿   ✿

We are ready to praise when all shines fair; but when life is overcast, when all things seem to be against us, when we are in fear for some cherished happiness, or in the depths of sorrow, or in the solitude of a life which has no visible support, or in a season of sickness, and with the shadow of death approaching,—then to praise God; then to say, This fear, loneliness, affliction, pain, and trembling awe are as sure tokens of love, as life, health, joy, and the gifts of home: "The Lord gave, and the Lord hath taken away," on either side it is He, and all is love alike; "blessed be the name of the Lord,"—this is the true sacrifice of praise. What can come amiss to a soul which is so in accord with God? What can make so much as one jarring tone in all its harmony? In all the changes of this fitful life, it ever dwells in praise.

Cardinal Henry Edward Manning

MEDITATIONS—XVII

. . . All *mankinde* is of one *Author*, and is one *volume;* when one Man dies, one *Chapter* is not *torne* out of the *booke*, but *translated* into a better *language;* and every *Chapter* must be so *translated; God* emploies several *translators;* some peeces are translated by *age*, some by *sicknesse*, some by *warre*, some by *justice*; but *God's* hand is in every *translation;* and his hand shall binde up all our scattered leaves againe, for that *Librarie* where every *booke* shall lie open to one another: As therefore the *Bell* that rings to a *Sermon*, calls not upon the *Preacher* onely, but upon the *Congregation* to come; so this *Bell* calls us all . . . Who casts not up his *Eye* to the *Sunne* when it rises? but who takes off his *Eye* from a *Comet* when that breaks out? Who bends not his *eare* to any *bell*, which upon any occasion rings? but who can remove it from that *bell*, which is passing a *peece of himselfe* out of this *world?* No man is an I*land*, intire of it selfe; every man is a peece of the *Continent*, a part of the *maine;* if a *Clod* bee washed away by the *Sea*, *Europe* is the *lesse*, as well as if a *Promontorie* were, as well as if a *Mannor* of thy *friends* or of *thine owne* were; any man's *death* diminishes *me*, because I am involved in *Man-*

21

kinde; And therefore never send to know for whom the *bell* tolls; It tolls for *thee* . . . *affliction* is a *treasure,* and scarce any man hath *enough* of it. No man hath *affliction* enough that is not matured, and ripened by it, and made fit for *God* by that *affliction.* If a man carry *treasure* in *bullion,* or in a *wedge* of *gold,* and have none coined into *currant Monies,* his *treasure* will not defray him as he travells. *Tribulation* is *Treasure* in the *nature* of it, but it is not *currant money* in the *use* of it, except wee get nearer and nearer our *home, Heaven,* by it.

John Donne

from THRENODY

Hearts are dust, hearts' loves remain;
Heart's love will meet thee again.

Revere the Maker; fetch thine eye
Up to his style, and manners of the sky.

Not of adamant and gold
Built he heaven stark and cold;
No, but a nest of bending reeds,
Flowering grass and scented weeds;
Or like a traveler's fleeing tent,
Or bow above the tempest bent;
Built of tears and sacred flames,
And virtue reaching to its aims;
Built of furtherance and pursuing,
Not of spent deeds, but of doing.

Silent rushes the swift Lord
Through ruined systems still restored,
Broadsowing, bleak and void to bless,
Plants with worlds the wilderness;
Waters with tears of ancient sorrow
Apples of Eden ripe tomorrow.

House and tenant go to ground,
Lost in God, in Godhead found.

Ralph Waldo Emerson

B. RELIGIOUS APPROACHES TO DEATH AND MOURNING

JUDAIC APPROACH TO DEATH AND MOURNING

Marvin Goldfine

All religions tend to view man's life and his death as an organic part of a grand pattern, divinely ordered, and endowed with an underlying purpose and meaning. That man's life, considered the climax of the divinely creative process, should be totally extinguished after a brief existence on earth seems most uncongenial to the religious mind. Whence developed the idea of immortality of the soul, a conception by no means confined to those with religious sensibilities or identification.

Judaism holds firmly to this view, though it eschews too precise a definition of the details involved. This world is seen as a vestibule to a grand celestial domain, where the righteous dwell eternally in a state of ecstasy derived from their close proximity to the source of divinity itself. Here the weary will find rest, the oppressed will be set free, and the virtuous granted their just reward.

Nevertheless, it is not a destination to be devoutly wished for. Death comes, but must be forestalled as long as possible. Life on earth is primary and decisive. It is here where man and society are challenged and put to the test. His work in the world is well within his power to perform, even if it is beyond his power to complete. There will always be others to follow who will carry on.

Thus death loses its sting to the extent that life is seen as a worthy and worthwhile endeavor. We mourn the loss of dear ones, friends, associates, leaders of communities and men of accomplishment, because they had enriched our lives and we are poorer without them. But mourning must have a stop, and after the period of grief appropriate to the situation, we return to our task—in life and in hope.

Traditional Judaism holds strongly to the view that since death knows no distinction as between persons, there should be a uniform type of casket for all funerals. The casket is to remain closed at all times, on the possible grounds that the living should be helped to remember the departed as they were in life rather than in death. While there is no requirement—nor need—to visit the funeral parlor

25

prior to the funeral, it is a religious command of importance to be present at the funeral and to visit the bereaved during the first week of mourning. One of the great acts of piety is concern for the burial of an unidentified or neglected deceased. Sages of old were known to leave their preoccupations in the academy in order to take personal charge in such instances.

Death is regarded in the Old Testament as the natural end for man, even as for all other species. There is a minimum of theorizing or philosophizing on the subject. True, its origin is attributed to Adam and Eve's lapse, but this is simply in keeping with Genesis' aim to set forth the origin of all observable things or events. Beyond this, there is little precise data of why men die, what death consists of, and what transpires after death.

This is not to suggest that death is not regarded in the Bible in all its tragic dimensions. It is, in fact, considered the supreme calamity that can befall man. It is meted out as the severest penalty for the most heinous crimes. Death is often seen as the just retribution for a life marked by sin and profanation of the name of the Lord. It is the consummation that men avoid, length of days being considered a blessing and a mark of virtue.

On the other hand, it is regarded as the state of final rest, where one is gathered unto "one's people" in peace and serenity. Descriptions of the demise of the patriarchs of Genesis suggest an attitude of both resignation and genuine grief in a way that endow them with a rare combination of grandeur and human pathos.

No book of the Old Testament echoes man's sentiments and inner life in such pure and lyrical form as does The *Book of Psalms.* It is said to contain the whole music of the heart of man, swept by the hand of the Maker. Heine remarked of this book that in its small compass it embodied all of "sunrise and sunset, birth and death, promise and fulfillment—the whole drama of humanity." Lamartine put it in these words—"Never has the soul opened before man and God in language so tender, so sympathetic and moving." No wonder, then, that it remains the most widely read of all biblical books, and the one most frequently used by those who seek reading that elevates and comforts. This end is achieved not only by its wide range of lofty ideas, but by a style and manner of expression that produce a mood of rich spiritual exaltation. It is that that accounts for its universal appeal among people of all cultures, all classes, or of widely-differing orientations to life.

The problems involved in arranging for a funeral are frequently faced up to by the mourners only after demise, and there are sometimes complexities which they are hardly in a state to cope with clearly. Here the undertaker can render invaluable advice and assistance in a general way.

However, there will always be questions of a particular nature that can only be answered by next of kin themselves. Should the funeral be arranged as soon as possible, or should some time be allowed to elapse to allow for full publicity, and for the arrival of relatives from distant places? Does the family feel impelled to "get it over with," or would they rather delay the final parting? Is time needed to seek and negotiate the purchase of a cemetery plot? These are examples of some questions that must be faced, and there are no true guidelines that can be universally applied, as each situation will require its own solution.

The death of an individual is an event that immediately disturbs the social balance of the community. It is the function of the funeral to work towards the correction of this unbalance. Certain things must be done. The body of the deceased must be given its final resting-place. The close relatives and friends must be helped to reorient themselves to the loss. The larger group—be they friends, acquaintances, fellow employees or neighbors—must have an accepted pattern of behavior or rite which will enable them to readjust to the new situation.

The funeral, then, ought to be arranged with only such delay as is necessary for the maximum achievement of the purposes mentioned. Some religious rulings — traditional Judaism, for instance — require burials on the same day as the death, or at the latest on the following day. In general, standard practice varies from 2 to 4 days after death occurs.

JUDAIC CUSTOMS AND ATTITUDES

Irwin Blank

We note in the legal material dealing with preparations for burying the dead, that the rabbis were very careful to insist that the arrangements be as simple and unburdensome as possible. Thus, the traditional coffin was a rude pine box and the burial shrouds were of simple linen. The thought was that the living had to go on living and that to assume financial costs and possibly debts because of funeral arrangements was an inappropriate tribute to the deceased and a disservice to the living. Although the practice of using a rude pine box is observed only amongst the most Orthodox Jews today, we would caution everyone concerning the inappropriate expenditure of large sums of money for funeral arrangements. This is not in keeping with Jewish tradition either for the affluent or those in moderate circumstances. It is far more appropriate to give money which may be available to charitable causes in memory of the deceased and in this way perpetuate his values and good name. Thus, we have also for some time been discouraging the purchasing and sending of floral arrangements and gift baskets of fruit, etc. We, instead, urge people to contribute to worthy causes in the name of the deceased.

It frequently happens that the mourners expect to receive immediate insights and comfort from the funeral service and the mourning period which follows. This seems to be particularly true with those whose ties with an ongoing religious pattern of life are nebulous at best. Those who expect immediate insights and comfort are frequently disappointed because they lack the necessary preparation for understanding the contents, the orientation and the purposes of the prayers and rituals. That is why it is important to make the time for a quiet discussion with one's rabbi about the nature of the prayers and the rituals in order to be guided in one's thinking and understanding. Making the opportunity for crystalizing one's spiritual orientation towards death and grief will be a source of comfort and strength.

Traditional practice discourages visiting the grave for a period of thirty days, and there is an inherent wisdom in this provision, for it guides the mourner to focus his attention on the living rather than to become morbidly preoccupied with the dead. It may well be that the provision which prohibits public displays of mourning on the Sabbath and festivals such as, not shaving, not bathing, and the wearing of torn garments, also communicates the importance of integrating death into a vital life rather than suppressing vital live in favor of death.

During the *Shiva* (seven day period of intense mourning immediately following burial) it is the practice for family and friends to visit the mourners in order to relieve them of their sense of isolation and deprivation. The mourners should not assume the role of hosts and hostesses and refreshments should not be served. While it is not necessary to maintain a funereal, depressed mood, certainly undo levity is inappropriate. Those gathered should make an effort to rehearse the virtues and the accomplishments of the deceased and thus begin the process of recognizing the finality of his physical death while appreciating the heritage of good memories which he has bequeathed to them.

DON'T

In the Talmud (Moed Katan 27b), and in the Code of Maimonides, we find the statement that it is the custom to make shrouds of fine white linen, but they must not be too costly. It is also a traditional practice that the coffin be a simple pine box. The underlying principle of these provisions has to do with the recognition that death is the great leveler, and that ultimately it is the spiritual values of life which give human existence its special distinction, rather than material accomplishment. Thus, both rich and poor face death with simplicity and dignity rather than with the status symbols of material acquisition. There is evidence that during the Roman period of Jewish history some people had elaborate sarcophagi, just as today some people spend considerable sums of money on coffins, shrouds, and burial arrangements. Of late, Boards of Rabbis of several communities have been concerned with the possibility that materialism and ostentatiousness were intruding upon the spiritual values to be derived from the confrontation of death. Therefore, they have begun campaigns to urge their congregants not to spend large sums of money on funeral arrangements in the mistaken notion that this constitutes a suitable tribute to the departed. Instead, they have urged that these funds should be used to support worthy community institutions and projects, thus perpetuating the memory of the departed in a more appropriate way.

With reference to mourning itself, we find that even in the period of deepest mourning, the *shiva* period, the mourner may change his clothes and put on everyday garments, and not maintain any public signs of mourning. Thus, grief too must have some bounds. In this case it is the Sabbath which places a limitation upon the expression of grief. Here we find that even in the midst of grief one is to hold onto the conviction that life has meaning and that one's spiritual commitment, as expressed through the observance of the Sabbath, has not lost its validity, even in the face of great personal tragedy. An additional prohibition has to do with the provision that one is not to visit the grave within thirty days after burial. Here, too, we find a defense against the possibility of establishing a morbid association with the grave and the deceased.

Of late, some of us have noticed the tendency of turning the *shiva* period—during which the mourners receive condolence calls from neighbors and friends—into a time for entertaining and socializing. Although it is clear that visiting, by its very nature, is a social experience, food and drink should not be served, and the mourners should certainly not consider themselves in the role of host or hostess. Visitors should keep their visits brief in order to avoid taxing the strength of the mourners; and, preferably, the conversation should be about the deceased and the particular memories which one has of him. The mourning period should provide an opportunity for the expression of grief and a sense of loss, but it should also provide the bridge to the resumption of normal activities, and the reconstruction of the life of the mourner.

REMEMBRANCE

I. YIZKOR

DIANE L. HERZ

Yizkor is the Hebrew word for "He shall remember." It is the first word of the prayer that gives its name to a special service of commemoration of the dead, conducted on only a few days during the year. The Day of Atonement at which the following sermons were delivered is one of these days. The Yizkor prayer is distinct from the Kaddish prayer recited at every service in praise of God's name.

Yizkor is a reminder of the whole of life; the debt owed by the living to keep the faith they were taught by those now dead. Yizkor serves as a reminder of the precious heritage of faith, and teaches that righteousness, charity and goodly works redeem man from death. Yizkor exhorts man to remember that the dead are to be recalled to memory not merely in an outpouring of grief but through deeds which ennoble life.

II.

"A TREE IS BEST MEASURED . . ."

NATHAN A. PERILMAN

The closing chapter of Carl Sandburg's monumental work on Abraham Lincoln is entitled, "A tree is best measured when it is down." Here Mr. Sandburg tells of the reaction in the United States and throughout the world to Mr. Lincoln's assassination. Not everyone spoke in the prophetic spirit of Edwin Stanton, who said, "Now he belongs to the ages." Some could not forget their harsh and cruel feelings toward the man who was swiftly destined to become America's greatest hero. But, for the most part, the reaction of the world was one of shock, horror, and uncontrollable grief.

"A tree is best measured when it is down" became a familiar proverb repeated in sermons, eulogies and editorials throughout the land.

33

People no longer thought of Lincoln's unpolished manner, his political attitudes, his simple, undenominational faith, and his behavior in the conduct of the war. While he had held his high position in life, they saw his human failings; but now, as he lay before them in death, they saw his great human virtues. They were beginning to see the complete man.

This is what we all do when a beloved one is taken from us; we see and understand him only when, like the tree, he is down. The faults we found difficult to live with, the failings we learned to overlook, the shortcomings which were part of his character, are forgotten; we see and we remember only the good. Let us thank God that He made us so, for had He not, memory might be unbearable. "De mortuis nil nisi bonum," said Plutarch, and we say it too: "concerning the dead, nothing but good."

Our religion enjoins us to remember our departed loved ones, to think of them in life's sacred moments, as they were when they were engaged in prayer, celebrating joy, or in time of trouble. Long after all else is forgotten by the indifferent and neglectful Jew, two words of our religious vocabulary remain vivid: Kaddish and Yizkor. But there are too many for whom this aspect constitutes the whole of Judaism. Though they deny themselves the joys and serenity and wisdom that they might draw from our ancient faith, they yet find much to cling to in its consolations.

As we read the simple but moving memorial service which has been designed for the most sacred hour of our holiest day, our departed will spring before our mind's eye for a little while and we shall see the qualities for which we have come to idealize them: the mother's sacrificial love; the father's protective strength; the sister's or brother's sweet companionship; the consecrated love of the husband or wife; the child's unspoiled devotion; the friend's constancy. We see only the full measure of the good as we see a tree when it is down; what the mind's eye sees, the heart will enshrine.

How wonderful memory is: it preserves in glowing colors the recollections we cherish; it obscures those experiences we would rather forget, and by its magic, it preserves our loved one as wholly good and altogether perfect.

Memory is a good thing. But there are none so tragic as those who wear the mantle of grief as if it were a coat of mail of which they cannot divest themselves, a coat of mail which is imprisoning from within and impenetrable from without. There are none so sad as the widowed, the orphaned, and the bereft to whom the urgencies of life and the passage of time can bring no consolation. It is not easy to measure the grief of another or to know how much a heart is broken. None of us is a stranger to sorrow, and we all know that there is no simple rule by which we can determine and weigh the amount of grief another should feel; yet, there are some for whom grief and tragedy become the all-absorbing concerns of life. Indeed, for such people, the sense of loss is so profound that even the image of their loved one is often obliterated because of preoccupation with the sorrow they bear in their hearts.

The inevitable effect of such preoccupation with sorrow is a withdrawal from life itself. Such people soon come to believe that no one can understand their heartache, and it is then but a short step to the conviction that theirs is a special kind of desolation. In extreme cases, their withdrawal from life is complete. They no longer want to be with the friends of a lifetime. The interests that absorbed them in a happier day begin to pall, their pursuits no longer have meaning, and they become like lost souls lurking in the shadows. This is tragic. Too often there is a deeper error that grows in the minds of those whose suffering is so profound: they think it is pious to suffer, that God ordains such self-rejection and self-hurt. But it is not so. God does not want to break our hearts—he gives us memory to make them whole again.

Psychologists tell us that much of our grief is bound up with feelings of guilt because we did not give more of ourselves to our loved ones during their lifetime. We feel guilty because there was unfinished business between us; because we did not deliver all the tokens of love that were due them; because we were more concerned with providing security for our loved ones than with giving ourselves to one another; because we were in search of a place among our friends and too little concerned with our place in the hearts of our loved ones. Our endless reasons for feeling guilty can be real enough, but very often they are meaningless.

The great truth which we must learn not only with our minds but with our hearts is that God intended life to go on; that our being here, even if bereft of our loved ones, has purpose and is part of a Divine plan. Though we cannot comprehend its vastness, we can fulfill the tasks to which God assigns us.

Since nature abhors a vacuum, we must also learn that life is not fully realized as long as the places our loved ones occupied are left vacant. The good they did, the kindness they showed, the charities they sustained, the values they supported, we, the living, must now carry on. Beyond this life we sense that there exists an immortality of the soul; we shall have to wait our time to learn what lies beyond. But there is an immortality we do know—that is, the living memorial of good deeds by which we perpetuate the lives of those who inspire them in us. There is no better way to lighten the heart's burden of grief, or to keep the memory of our loved ones always fresh.

On this day, when we give thought to our departed, and whenever we contemplate the mystery and wonder of life, let us be thankful that when God gave us a fragment of His omniscience, He withheld for Himself the secret of life and death. For had He shared it with us, it would be too much for us to bear. It is far easier for us to live with this mystery than to attempt to penetrate it. Let us thank God for memory, for memory makes it possible for us to lick the sweet spoon of life again and again. More than in any other living experience, in a time of death we must depend on faith and trust. In unison with the poet whose song of praise we sing to the glory of God in the Adon Olam, we must say, "Into thy hand I commend my spirit, both when I sleep and when I wake, and with my spirit my body too; God is with me; I shall not fear."

III.

JACOB PHILIP RUDIN

As the wise word has it: "It is with sorrows, as with countries: each man has his own." All of us are together, yet each of us is alone, each heart knowing its own solitude of separation. Hans Zinsser has written: "At times the dead are closer to us than the living, and the wisdom and affection of the past stretch blessing hands over our lives, projecting a guardian care out of the shadows and helping us over hard places. For there are certain kinds of love that few but the very wise fully understand until they have become memories."

Yizkor is such an hour of closeness between the living and the dead, when wisdom and affection stretch blessing hands over our lives; and when love, now become memory, rests as benediction upon us. Here is where the pain lies: when we think upon the time when love was an ever-present reality and not the memory into which death transforms it, when we sometimes took that love for granted and let a thoughtless word, an unaccomplished deed, make that love less than it should have been.

Yizkor says this to us, not to build up remorse or guilt, but to teach us. Death clarifies: the unimportant is stripped away and the meaningless cast aside. Death clarifies: so that love, become memory, is life's proper setting.

Yizkor is for letting the music come back, softly and sweetly. Yizkor is to hush us and to heal us, because we are very tired under the burden which death has brought. Yizkor is to hush us with the quiet strength of prayer. Yizkor is to heal us with the wisdom that death gives urgency to life. Then sit quiet, without bitter tears, and let the silence flow in, bringing more love than grief, more gratitude than rebellion.

In Cologne, on the wall of a cellar which had once been a prison, there was found this inscription: "I believe in the sun, even when it is not shining. I believe in love, even when feeling it not. I believe in God even when He is silent." So God's spirit abides, in love, in memory, in the reality of this world, in the reality of the human spirit.

Over one of the entrances to the Cathedral of Milan, there is carved a rose and the inscription, "Beauty fadeth and wasteth away." Over a second entrance, there is chiseled a sword, and the inscription, "Pain ends at last and is no more." Over the central entrance, there is carved a lamp and the words, "But the things of the spirit are for everlasting life."

What are these things? To touch life with beauty. To reach forth our healing hands to another's pain. To speak the comforting word to another bereaved, because we ourselves have walked through the valley. These are the gifts of the spirit which are for everlasting life. If your loved ones gave them to you, then weep not. Your inheritance is cast in the frame of immortality.

Yizkor is the reminder of those who sleep and who are not dead. May they sleep secure. May they, in the deepest sense, never be among the dead, but always among the sleeping ones whose slumber we guard with our affection.

Weep not, then, for your loved ones. Weeping is not for those who are remembered. Tears are for those who are forgotten. This is the hour of Yizkor, remembrance time, when affection, deepened by loss becomes more precious, and dear ones, sleeping, touch our lives in benediction. Amen.

IV.

JACOB K. SHANKMAN

When I was a lad at school it was customary for the teacher every day to write a proverb or adage on the blackboard. We had to memorize those sayings and in time we accumulated quite a collection of them. I still remember with pleasure, "Early to bed and early to rise makes a man healthy, wealthy and wise," or "Cast your bread upon the waters and it will return to you after many days." Paradoxically, as we grew up, we noticed that the proverb was not always accurate or true; in fact, the reverse was often more true. Going to bed early made you none of the promised things; the waters did not return your bread. The converse and opposite of the proverb was true.

It is in this spirit that I recall the saying, "Dead men tell no tales." How wrong it is. Dead men *do* tell tales. In the holiness of a memorial hour, when we come together to remember those we have lost, and the words of Shelley are tenderly true, "music, when soft voice die, vibrates in the memory," we know, incontrovertibly, that dead men do tell tales and they make music.

In every person there is a private shrine of memory and love, and in that sanctuary our loved ones abide. We sense their presence, caress their spirits, and enfold them in our hearts. They talk to us; they tell tales. Thus the pain of separation is soothed by memory, the hurt sustained is healed by love; and we ourselves become purified and ennobled through our sorrow.

What tales these memories tell! I recall my earliest encounter with death. One of my boyhood companions had a rheumatic heart. He also had uncanny control of a baseball, and could throw strikes with amazing consistency. We couldn't understand the restrictions on physical exertion imposed by his solicitous parents. We would play chess and collect stamps, but we also played baseball and he *pitched*. He was just emerging from his teens when that weak heart could beat no more. Now many years have passed, but the tale of boyhood activities and laughter, and of common experiences and pranks, warms the crannies of memory and touches my heart with a soothing benediction.

I recall another friend, too. We were friends at Seminary and through the early years of our Rabbinate. What fun we had together and what problems we wrestled with! He had all the gifts that made him superior: a brilliant mind, a retentive memory, a voice that was golden and eloquent, a ready and keen wit, abundant humor, perceptive insights into human beings, boundless compassion. He had everything and he gave friendship and love. He wrote a book called *Peace of Mind* which gave light and understanding to millions of readers. Joshua Loth Liebman died when he was only forty-one, but what a tale my memories of him tell.

I recall my parents, and what tales they told me! Memories of stories told by my father of an old world, of traditions that came out of the vast literary store-house of our history and faith; memories of walking to our house of worship with him and of praying by his side; memories of whippings I got while learning to be truthful, honest, and obedient; memories of tears and laughter. And memories of Mother, poring over the Bible or energetically preparing for the Holy Days or singing in that sweet soprano voice the Songs of Schumann. Tell no tales? As long as consciousness is within me, the stories will be heard again and again, as they come back to warm my spirit, heal my soul and bless me.

And the teachers I recall, long since gone to their rest, who taught me to put letters and syllables together and then to see the wonder of the word and the marvel of the poem. I remember my French teacher. She hobbled and limped and when she spoke she spat saliva through her buck teeth; she was probably as ugly a woman as can be imagined. But her eyes flamed with the eagerness to impart her knowledge and she allowed no nonsense on the way to learning; she made it a serious but a glorious adventure. Tell no tales? She wanted you to learn, and you did.

These are the warm memories and the intimate, personal tales that are told. But there are many more. It is fashionable in our age to downgrade the New England poets who were the glory of America's literary tradition in the nineteenth century. They are considered regional, sentimental, undistinguished. Yet I feel that what they had to say is enduringly true, in our days as it was in theirs. One of Longfellow's poems was entitled *A Psalm of Life*. We had to memorize the words in which Longfellow affirmed that dead men tell tales. He wrote:

"Lives of great men all remind us | We can make our lives sublime,|
And, departing, leave behind us, | Footprints on the sands of time;"
A blasé, sophisticated, troubled and disillusioned generation needs to recapture that mood, for its own sanity.

We could rehearse the lives of all the benefactors of humanity and perceive the truth of those lines. Henry J. Kaiser died not long ago; he was the builder of a giant industrial empire, who made ships and cars, roads and factories. And he once said, "I always have to dream up against the stars. If I don't dream I'll make it, I won't even get close." He dreamed and told his tale. Carl Sandburg was a folk-singer and poet of the people. He was a disciple and biographer of Lincoln, and like him, he admired the common man. He knew that "dreams are stronger than death." How poignantly he could write of a mother's love for her child, and what a tale it tells:

"I love you," | said a great mother. |

"I love you for what you are, | knowing so well what you are. |

And I love you more yet, child, | deeper yet than ever, child, |
    for

What you are going to be, | knowing so well you are going far, | knowing

Your great works are ahead, | ahead and beyond, | yonder and far over yet."

These tales are endless. Listen to them. They may be personal or they may affect all of us, but dead men tell tales—tales of love and friendship; of kindness and sympathy, of hope and faith, of suffering and compassion, of bright achievement and infinite blessing.

Such tales comfort us not only in the holiness of a memorial hour, but at all times when our ears are open to hear. We cannot bring our loved ones back, but through these tales they remain with us forever and we commune with them. They have not been taken away; they are with us now, and the reason they are with us, close in mind and heart, is that they never stopped telling these tales. They faced life with steadfastness and courage and blessed us with their devotion and love. And even as they blessed us, so must we emerge from our pain and longing for them and strengthen ouselves for the tasks and challenges of today and for the hopes and promise of tomorrow, for we, too, will have tales to tell in our turn.

This is the lesson, the blessing, the comfort and the promise of a hallowed memorial hour. Dead men tell tales. They never stop.

V.

DAVID J. SELIGSON

"Thou shalt be missed because thy seat will be empty." These are the words of Jonathan, the son of King Saul, addressed to David, whom his father regarded as his arch-enemy and the threat to his rulership. This was how Jonathan expressed his love for the man whom his father had sworn to kill. It was not a passing comment but a deep and sincere expression of true friendship. David was to leave Jonathan's presence. His life was in danger; the two friends did not know whether they would meet again; and in his anxiety for his friend's safety, Jonathan gave voice to his concern in a way which each of us who has known bereavement can feel: "Thou shalt be missed because thy seat will be empty."

It is in the very nature of human society that the civilized human being lives amidst his fellows, and the most tender of these human associations is the family group. Unhappy and incomplete indeed is the life of a man who has not felt the need for this kind of association. Having achieved it, he knows what a blessing it is. Whether for good or evil, for joy or sorrow, a man lives in the company of those he loves. We become accustomed to their presence; when they have gone from our sight, we miss them, we feel the void in our lives. "Thou shalt be missed because thy seat will be empty." There is no one here who has not felt the sharp pang at the thought that one with whom life was shared, its joys and sorrows, has passed from sight for all time. We miss him because his seat is empty. A link in the family circle has been broken. Time, far from erasing the memory of those we have lost, has enhanced it. It has invested them with a quality of the spirit so that we think of them only as we knew them at their best. We treasure every kind word they spoke, every noble deed they performed, and are grateful for the wealth of love and devotion which their personalities added to our lives.

At a time like this, it is only natural that we should ask ourselves what fate will be ours when we have joined them. No one can peer behind the veil of the future life, and yet none of us can face with complacency the desolate thought that we should be completely forgotten in the hearts of those of whose lives we have been a part. We cannot believe that where we have been there will be only a void and a nothingness. In our innermost hearts, we should like to think that we, too, shall be missed by someone, somewhere. Our way in life must be guided by the same three-fold principle that has enshrined the lives of our dear ones in our own hearts: word, act and personality. Great words are deathless. They are treasured by the centuries and those who spoke them are unforgotten in the annals of men.

It is not given to all of us to say great words, but within our own spheres of influence, small though they may be, we may yet be remembered for the good word of cheer, of friendliness, for the encouragement that we may tender to others by sympathy and understanding for them in their hour of need.

Actions, deeds of loving-kindness and mercy, are milestones in human progress. In the recent hostilities in the Middle East, a little Jordanian girl was brought to a hospital in Jerusalem in a most critical condition. Clinically she was dead. Her jugular vein had been pierced by a bullet. Her case seemed hopeless. All the resources of the hospital were marshalled to save her. Physicians, surgeons and nursing staff worked round the clock. Today, she has been restored to her family, alive and well.

Great acts of great souls shine like beacons in the annals of men. Each of us may be remembered ultimately by "little, nameless, unremembered acts of kindness and of love." From day to day, we can bring to others a measure of happiness, the benison of knowing that they have not been forgotten.

Personality is a thing that is hard to define. It is something that cannot be bestowed by wealth, education, or position. Some people radiate great power of personality, and to experience it brings a certain feeling of happiness, a warmth and cordiality. Perhaps it might be described as a kind of humanness, a combination of qualities which makes a man unforgettable in the memories of those who knew him.

Tender memories fill our hearts as we think of whose words, actions, and personalities enriched our lives. This hour we pay humble tribute to thoughts that are ever with us, and to silent reflections that linger ever amidst the toil and turmoil of life. From the thought of them, let us receive that hallowed inspiration that will serve as a beacon as we proceed on our way in life.

VI.

DAVID R. BLUMENTHAL

Renoir, the great French artist, suffered from rheumatism in his hands during the later years of his life. He painted by being placed in a chair, which was moved as he directed. As he applied the paint to the canvas, suffering intensely, perspiration covered his brow. Yet he persisted and continued to paint masterpieces. One day Matisse, his disciple, pleaded, "Why torture yourself to do more?" Gazing at his favorite canvas, Renoir replied, "The pain passes, but the beauty remains." We can learn much about life from this beautiful story, for it teaches us that life, if it is to be beautiful, requires dedication, effort, and courage even in the face of great hardship.

This principle—that life, if it is to be beautiful, sometimes requires of us dedication, effort, and even courage—holds true in our lives. I recall a story told me by a colleague. He had been visiting some relatives who were in their eighties. While there, he noticed that the man of the house committed a "faux pas" in table manners and that his wife immediately corrected him. My friend was upset to think of someone's being henpecked at over eighty years of age. I tried to explain to him that he was not being henpecked at all, but that all this was part of the game of love and life, that the husband had probably purposely committed the "faux pas" to provoke his wife into a little show of attention, and, in its own way, that this was really a beautiful thing to see—a couple, advanced in years, still in love enough to play these little games. I commented, too, that their life must also have been painful for it to have been so beautiful. Much of the pain has passed, but the beauty has remained. They have lived their lives with as much dedication, effort, dignity, and courage in the face of the hardships and difficulties of life as they were able, and the beauty remains. So it is, I think, with the memories we have of those who have passed on: if these memories are to become and *remain* beautiful, we will be called upon to overcome certain hardships, we will have to put forth dedication, effort, and even courage. Each of us must endure courageously the pain of mourning—the depression, the anger, the sadness, the tears, the sense of being all alone, and of having to face the world alone—for, only after we have done the work of mourning, will the memories begin to be beautiful, only after the pain has passed away, will the beauty begin to remain. To *preserve* that beauty, each of us will have to live up to the values, aspirations, and hopes of those who have passed on. We will have to cherish the beauty of the family life they started and, to do that, we will have to undergo the pain of keeping doors open, of maintaining relationships, and of making peace when the need arises. We will have to cherish the beauty of friendships they developed. And we will have to cherish the love of *our* children and, to do that, we will have to undergo the pain of letting them reject that which we may hold very dear. We will have to permit them to make their own mistakes, including the big ones, and we will always have to give selflessly of our time and effort. Life and memories can be beautiful, but not without dedication, effort, pain, and courage. "The pain passes, but the beauty remains."

VII.

WALTER JACOB

. . . Old sorrows fill us again and again. It does not matter whether our beloved left us many years ago or during the past year, for grief again rises within us each time we recite our traditional words of mourning. We mourn again, but we are doing far more than that. We are making a public declaration of willingness to accept a fact of our life. We accept it because we have no choice. No matter how tragic, no matter how sudden, no matter how difficult, death must be accepted.

. . . Without this acknowledgment we look at life and believe that everything is there solely for our benefit, and we take it very much for granted. We looked upon life in this fashion when we were children and many of us continue to view it in this manner.

. . . We do not willingly accept many of the obstacles of life. But after a while we begin to acknowledge our physical limitations, our emotional limits, and our intellectual boundaries; and we try to remain within them.

. . . Take your frustrations, all your difficulties and see them in the light of a Day of Remembrance. Remember them well, but recall them only to be able to forget them.

. . . Our prayers show us a path through which we may overcome many of the frustrations of our life. We need not feel useless; we need not be overwhelmed. The road is clear if we accept the past and revive our dreams. . . . The memory of those dear to us often moves us to action. Let memory move us down the right road. Let it lead us until we are able to walk alone. Let it well up in our hearts. May it open portals of hope and not misery, fulfillment and not frustration; may it open portals of blessing—God's blessing!

EXCERPTS FROM THE PRAYER BOOK OF *REFORM JUDAISM*

1. All you who mourn the loss of loved ones, and, at this hour, remember the sweet companionship and the cherished hopes that have passed away with them, give ear to the word of comfort spoken in the name of God. Only the body has died, and has been laid in the dust. The spirit lives in the shelter of God's love and mercy. Our loved ones continue, also, in the remembrance of those to whom they were precious. Their deeds of loving-kindness, the true and beautiful words they spoke, are treasured up as incentives to conduct by which the living honor the dead. And when we ask in our grief: Whence shall come our help and our comfort? then in the strength of faith let us answer with the Psalmist: My help cometh from God. He will not forsake us nor leave us in our grief. Upon Him we cast our burden and He will grant us strength according to the days He has apportioned to us. All life comes from Him; all souls are in His keeping. Come then, and in the midst of sympathizing fellow-worshipers, rise and hallow the name of God.

2. In nature's ebb and flow, God's eternal law abides. When tears dim our vision and grief clouds our understanding, we often lose

sight of His eternal plan. Yet we know that growth and decay, life and death, all reveal His purpose. He who is our support in the struggles of life is also our hope in death. We have set Him before us and shall not despair. In His hands are the souls of all the living and the spirits of all flesh. Under His protection we abide and by His love are we comforted. O Life of our life, Soul of our soul, cause Thy light to shine into our hearts, and fill our spirit with abiding trust in Thee.

3. O Thou who givest life and ordainest death, we trust in Thee. Even when those we love enter into the shadow of death, our faith in Thee does not falter. For surely Thou wilt not abandon us to despair, nor those we love to the eternal midnight of the tomb. Thou hast placed man upon the earth, bestowed upon him a mind to seek truth, a heart to perceive love and beauty, and Thou wilt not crush it all forever. Our life is more than a watch in the night, than yesterday when it is past, for Thou dost establish the work of Thy hands. Dust we are, and unto dust we return, but the spirit born of Thy spirit, breathed into the clay to animate and to ennoble, returns unto Thee, the Fountainhead of all spirits. Thou art in the setting as in the rising sun, in our bereavements as in our blessings, and Thine everlasting arms uphold us in the vicissitudes of life and in our lone journey through the valley of shadows.

Teach us then, O Father, to speak with all our hearts the words, hallowed by centuries of faith. Trust us to acknowledge Thy sovereignty and Thy wisdom with perfect trust that death is but the portal unto eternal life.

Let us, then, give praise unto God who is the source of our salvation and our abiding hope.

4. When cherished ties are broken and fond hopes shattered, only faith and confidence can lighten the heaviness of the heart. The pang of separation is hard to bear, but to brood over our sorrow is to embitter our grief.

The Psalmist said that in his affliction he learned the law of God. Indeed, not unavailing will be our grief, if it send us back to serve and bless the living. We learn how to counsel and comfort those who, like ourselves, are sorrow-stricken. Though absent, the departed still minister to our spirits, teaching us patience, faithfulness and devotion. Within the circle of daily association, we often failed to discern their worth and their loveliness. In the remembrance of their virtues and affections, the best and purest part of their nature lies eternally enshrined. Let us lift our head in hope, and summon our strength for duty. We dwell in the shelter of the Almighty, for He is our refuge and our fortress.

5. The Lord giveth, the Lord taketh away, blessed be the name of the Lord. As we recall the beloved ones who have passed away, these words bring healing to the hurt that death has wrought. Our loved ones have answered the summons that sounds for all men, for we are sojourners upon earth and our times are in His hands. We loose our hold upon life when our time is come, as the leaf falls from the bough when its day is done. The needs of the righteous enrich the lives of men as the fallen leaf enriches the soil beneath. The dust returns to the earth, the spirit lives on with God's eternal years. Like the stars by day, our beloved dead are not seen with mortal eyes, but they shine on in the untroubled firmament of endless time. Let us be thankful for the companionship that continues in love that is stronger than death and spans the gulf of the grave. Cherishing their memory, let us, in the presence of the congregation, sanctify the name of God.

6. We are assembled with our friends in the shadow that has fallen on their home. We raise our voices together in prayer to the Father above, asking for comfort and strength. We need light when gloom darkens our home; whence can it come but from the Creator of light? We need fortitude and resignation under the chastening of the Lord; whence can these come save from Him who lays the burden upon us? Who among us has not passed through trials and bereavements! Some bear fresh wounds in their hearts and therefore feel the more keenly the kinship of sorrow. Others, whose days of mourning are more remote, still recall the comfort that sympathy brought to their sorrowing hearts. And those of us who have not yet tasted of the bitter cup cannot know how soon we may be called on to drink of it. All that we prize is but lent to us and we must surrender it when

God demands. We are travelers on the same road, which leads to the same end.

7. At thy command, O God, we have laid to rest a dearly beloved one. We murmur not at Thine inscrutable decree; we pray for strength to bear what Thou hast laid on us. Let Thy light shine on us in the night of our sorrow that we may find the path of life and follow it towards the goal which Thou hast appointed to each of Thy children. We thank Thee for the life which in Thy goodness Thou hadst given and in Thy wisdom hast taken away. Make us to know Thy ways that in our love we may triumph over grief and despair; calm Thou our troubled spirits that athwart our tears may arch the rainbow of Thine eternal promise. Praised be Thou, O Lord, who comfortest the mourners. Amen.

CHRISTIAN FAITH AND DEATH—SELECTED READINGS

ROBERT B. REEVES, JR.

Come unto me and I will give you rest.

(Matthew 11:28)

See . . . how faithfully the Lord is leading thee to true peace who surroundeth thee with so many crosses. It is called "the peace of God, which passeth all understanding"; that is, which is not known by feeling or perception or thinking. All our thinking cannot attain nor understand it; none but those who of free will take up the cross laid on them, those tried and troubled in all they feel and think and understand, afterward experience this peace.

(Martin Luther)

God grant me the serenity
to accept the things I cannot
change; courage to change
the things I can; and
wisdom to know the difference.

(Reinhold Niebuhr)

Lord, make me an instrument of your peace
Where there is hatred . . . let me sow
love

Where there is injury . . . pardon.

Where there is doubt . . . faith.

Where there is despair . . . hope.

Where there is darkness . . . light.

Where there is sadness . . . joy.

O Divine Master, grant that I may not so
much seek

To be consoled . . . as to console,

To be understood . . . as to understand

To be loved . . . as to love,
For

It is in giving . . . that we receive.

It is in pardoning, that we are pardoned,

It is in dying . . . that we are born to
eternal life.

(St. Francis of Assisi)

Do not look forward to what might happen tomorrow; the same everlasting Father who cares for you to-day will take care of you to-morrow, and every day. Either He will shield you from suffering, or He will give you unfailing strength to bear it. Be at peace then, and put aside all anxious thoughts and imaginations.

(St. Francis de Sales)

SUMMARY OF A CHRISTIAN'S BELIEFS

GORDON K. BLUNT

The soul does survive the death of the body.
God cares for the soul after it has passed from this life to the next.
Help, here and now, is available. The fellowship of the church is important to the sorrowing and is available.

Prayer is a vital force.

Discussion and sharing of feelings is helpful.

A CONTINUATION

Robert A. Edgar

When grief strikes, some people feel that they should change their whole way of life. They should sell the home, go to another climate, try to escape the past. How tragic this is. Those who die ahead of us want us to carry on as before. Think of our need for friends who know us. How important it is to stay near them!

How important it is to rejoice in memories. It is difficult at first. Go to the familiar holiday spot as usual. There will be a terrific lonesomeness for a while, but soon this will give way to the feeling that you are not alone. *Now* it is all right to feel his presence because you have gone through the fantasy/reality stage and you know that his presence is real. And sometimes this feeling of his presence is more real than some of the other experiences which are so important to us.

WHAT IS HAPPENING TO FEELINGS?

Edgar N. Jackson

Much of life's richest experience is closely bound up with deep feelings. If we were to lose our capacity to feel deeply, life would be sadly impoverished. Yet students of the personality sciences raise a warning that we are in just such danger. Much of the sentiment that has surrounded life is being eroded away, and little that is adequate is being substituted for it.

There are at least three reasons why changes are taking place that affect our attitude toward our feelings. First is the current trend toward intellectualization. Second is the modification of the values that are prevalent in our culture. Third is the commercialization and abuse of feelings and the resistance against these practices.

During the last few decades, an attitude has found acceptance among many people that we should not show our feelings when we meet life crises, but rather should calmly try to think them through. In fact, some psychologists have implied that feelings are a form of disease to be isolated and controlled. People who express their feelings openly and honestly are suspect; and those who want to be respected as well-balanced and mature are obliged to repress their feelings and express them only in private, if at all.

This attitude has become apparent in many ways, but we can illustrate it from the political, social, and religious experience of people. All too often, for example, the intellectual looks at the international scene and, after examining all of the aspects of a problem, tries to analyze them objectively. There is nothing wrong with objective analysis in and of itself, but to approach the important problems of life with nothing but objectivity can be hazardous. The mood of superficial optimism that often characterizes the thinking of the intellectual is dangerous because he is trying to avoid the problems that disruptive emotions produce. There can be no clear thinking without making allowance for emotions, for there are no emotions that do not color thinking. To deny this basic fact of the mental processes is to jeopardize the very resources the intellectual seeks to glorify.

It is difficult to think of religious experience without an emotional response to beauty, truth, and goodness. Often this is shown in the acts of worship and the ceremonial events that are a traditional part of worship. But now, we see the more specifically intellectual approaches to religion expressing themselves in a denial of the validity of rites, rituals, and ceremonials. It is interesting to note that the reform movements relating to the religious and social events surrounding death bring together in a common cause the atheists, who deny religion as a valid part of life, and the intellectuals, who tend to deny a place for strong feelings. In a common resistance to strong feelings, they support the psychologically unsound aspects of a death-denying, death-defying cultural mood.

What is observed in thinking that denies feeling is also apparent in a change in the basic values prevalent in our culture. Increasingly, we focus attention on youth, health, and physical vigor and turn our eyes away from the painful, the ugly, and the aged as if these conditions were not a part of life. But in order to do this we have to ignore or eliminate significant aspects of reality.

When a prevalent attitude toward human experience tends to deny or ignore important parts of that experience, the philosophy of life that emerges is distorted. This distortion shows up in an increased focus on what is *acceptable,* with an attendant disregard for the rest of life. Life therefore becomes increasingly centered upon the present with its satisfactions, and plays down the past and the future. The past with its accumulated experience is ignored as irrelevant to the present, and we say, "History is bunk." Also, we look away from those aspects of the future that may be incompatible with our quest for satisfaction in the present. This in turn tends to undercut responsibility for the consequences of present actions. Thus we undermine the very basis for ethical action. The resultant reduction of life to a concern for the present undermines the very qualities that have made man unique—a sense of history that has been the foundation for learning and an ethical interest in the future that has conditioned behavior in the present.

To limit life to a preoccupation with the present tends to make religion irrelevant. For the roots of ethical religion grow from a concern for the future, and the meaning of faith finds expression in a way of life that is rooted in the past and concerned about the future. What good does it do to talk about tradition and responsibility to people who are concerned primarily with the satisfactions of the present?

This breakdown of the value structure is fortified by the direct and indirect selectivity of our educational processes, for the values that underlie education are closely correlated with the purposes of education. Education is used to support the prevailing point of view in our culture. We see what we want to see, and teach what we feel verifies what we want to believe. Indirect education through recreation and entertainment makes death seem trivial and life itself as two-dimensional as the television or motion picture screen upon which it moves. Our children are brought up in an atmosphere of shallow values and a warped idea of the basic realities that have traditionally given structure to living.

Not only is life contracted into the present, not only are the values by which to live treated lightly, and religion made increasingly irrelevant, but also the exponents of a return to reality, sound religion, and moral values are held up to ridicule as the unwanted remnants of a way of thinking that has been wisely outgrown. Old ways of doing things are cast off with little effort to understand them, and with no apparent desire to create adequate substitutes. As some researchers have pointed out, the therapeutic resources of rites, rituals, and ceremonials are abandoned with no recognition of the fact that they help people work through feelings that are too deep and powerful to put into words. This abandonment is hazardous, for in the place of useful ways of acting out our conflicts, we find only morbidity of spirit, maladaptive behavior, and an atrophy of the capacity to love. Emotions are like muscles; unused, they become flabby and weak.

Assaults are made upon the emotions by those who would use them for commercial purposes. Sex, which can be the basis for the most significant communication of deep feelings between two persons, has been debased to a gimmick to sell everything from mouthwash to automobiles. Little wonder that this saturation in trivial sex has created a generation of young people whose superficial characteristics are so indistinct that it takes a very careful look sometimes to distinguish a girl from a boy.

Commercialization of the funeral has aroused negative reactions in many persons. Much of the criticism is directed against the selling practices that appeal to maudlin sentimentality. True sentiment is far deeper than sentimentality, and the deepest feelings cannot be resolved by merely doing nice things for the deceased. The funeral can and should be a most valued means for the expression of these feelings, for it is a significant part of the practices surrounding the bereaved.

It is easily demonstrable that the more ceremonial events there are at the time of an emotional crisis, the more easily persons move through the crisis in healthful ways. Denied these outlets for the emotions, they can develop deep wounds and emotional scars that may well take years to heal.

If our capacity to feel deeply about the important things of life withers away, it will be the result of unbalanced intellectualizations which ignore feelings, the result of the demolition of a value structure that recognizes the sacredness of life and everything that is related to its finest expression, and the result of the commercialization of the channels of emotional expression that in turn tend to atrophy the very emotions they seek to serve.

BENEFITS OF RELIGION: *UNITY*

GLENN R. MOSLEY

Religious beliefs are not a substitute for grief; they should be a vehicle for its healthful expression. In the main, the Church's customs concerning death are society's evolved customs. Society evolves traditions and customs according to its own needs. The sharing of grief with friends and other loved ones is a custom with a wisdom all its own.

A religious service should lift the attention from death, not by denying it, but by helping to fit it into a larger perspective. It should emphasize the importance of a living faith that can give courage in the present and direction for the future. It should provide evidence of group strength available to the individual who is weakened by sorrow and in need of the strength of others. The religious service should recognize the dignity of life and the validity of people's feelings in the face of death. All who enter into such a service help to support those who are grieving.

Not only by what is said and done to uphold the bereaved in a religious ceremony, but by every word and act, the whole community of man shares in sustaining the bereaved. It is important that the community support and accept the emotions of the bereaved, confirm the reality of the loss, and give assurance for the future.

Since prolonged grief can lead to or be symptomatic of serious illness, it is important that we learn ways to manage it rather than be dominated by it. In closing this chapter, we list here two suggestions for just such management.

First, we must determinedly resist circuitous routes around the truth, and face the painful task of accepting the full reality of what has happened. There is no known easy way to face the death of one who was deeply loved, so we need courage to endure the pain. We need also to know that ours is a healthy pain, one that brings with it its own healing.

The second phase of change is to begin finding ways to use some of the strengths gained in our relationship with the person who has died. For example, parents invest their hope in the life of a child. If the child passes on, they must withdraw that hope in order to look toward the future realistically. Adult children cannot foster dependent feelings any longer when their aged parents die, or they will be clinging to a false security. It is important that the bereaved individual develop ways that will make it possible to find new interests and satisfactions, positive, constructive, and creative activities. The bereaved must make new relationships and acquaintances. Although memories of the past may be treasured, one cannot live wholesomely on memories alone; one's creative energies must be planted in areas where they can bear fruit.

The bereaved needs to have those around him who can help him to accept both his distraught emotions and the reality of his loss. He needs relatedness to a responsible person to help him regain assurance for the future. After years of training and experience in helping others meet the loss of a loved one, I find it is still best for the bereaved to seek out someone who will put his arms around him, who will let him literally "cry on his shoulder" if he wants or needs to, who will give him either verbal or tacit assurance of being cared about, and who will, in time, retreat.

CHURCH OF THE TRUTH AND GRIEF

Erwin Seale

It is important to realize that grief is a meaningful emotion. Don't try to stifle grief. Let the tears flow. Let the heart empty itself. Grief and rapture are poles between which the soul is stretched and exercised that she may know herself apart and distinct from what she feels. The time of grief is a growing time. All the words that we say or that are said to us are hollow and unreal. The only truth in the hour of death is silence and rest. For when someone we love gets off at a certain stopping place and the train moves on without him or her, we cannot understand; therefore we must trust and rest. The shock of death is like any other shock—it unnerves us and stops our accustomed ways. Like the returning sensation to a benumbed limb, life, movement, and interest will come again after rest and recuperation. The same healing power which restores the injured limb will heal the troubled heart. Out of grief will come deeper insight and richer meaning. When a limb or an organ of the body, such as an arm, an eye, or a kidney, is lost, the other gains a double measure of strength. So, too, when a beloved member of the family goes on ahead, those who are left behind receive an extra share of life and strength, courage, and grace. The dead bequeath more than their earthly possessions to the living.

There is nearly always the problem of guilt. "If only I had known," or "If I had been there" or "if I had done this or that"—these and other recurring thoughts are, like death itself, well nigh universal in the experience of those who grieve. Regret and remorse are signs of growth, however. "Make the most of your regrets," says Thoreau, "to regret deeply is to live afresh." It is useless to punish oneself now for what one might have done earlier. If we had known better, we should have done better. He who knows better now is not quite the same person who did not know previously. Besides, there is a good deal of pride and egotism in regret and remorse. They rest on the supposition that an act of ours was so important that what we failed to do was fateful.

In the dark hours after death, every memory is torture, and if you forget for one blessed moment of relief, you quickly reproach your-

61

self for your callousness. The sight of a garment or a book or a toy brings constriction of the muscles and a flood of tears. In all of this you will suppose your are thinking of your beloved. Actually, you are thinking of your loss. You may actually be feeling sorry for yourself and resenting his going ahead or resenting heaven for allowing it. As a widow said to me, "I feel that God is implacable." There is selfishness in prolonged grief. Grief is real and grief is important but it must pass to higher things—to insights and spiritual growth.

It is important in time of death to turn quickly to life again. As a husband "heard" his deceased wife say to him, "For my sake turn to life again. Complete the dear, unfinished tasks of mine. Therein I may comfort you." We erect monuments of stone and bronze to our dear departed when all that is required is that we live the better now for their having been with us and so make our lives monuments and memorials of their life in us. One of the noblest reactions to death I ever heard was from the lips of a wife as she turned from her husband-physician's grave: "I am glad that I could be the one to survive and bear this sorrow for him."

A period of being alone after death is in order. Take time to accept, review, and revise and then go on. Just as a driver who has had an accident must immediately drive again lest the patterns of shock, fear and inadequacy settle in the mind, so must the survivor return to his labors and interests.

He must make his peace with the facts of death. He may consider that anything so universal as death cannot be basically bad, and that while those who read this are drawing their latest breath, others are drawing their last and still others are drawing their first and so the cycle of life goes on, minute by minute, hour by hour and year by year. It is the going and the coming of the One Being.

Our beloved came into this life as a little baby. How young and fresh and new he was. But look again! He was not unlike a wrinkled old man! The child was old before he was young. "Trailing clouds of glory do we come from God who is our home." And the poet asks the baby, "Where did you get that little tear?" And the baby answers, "I found it waiting when I got here." Here the blithe spirit meets the world of matter or form, of illusions and confusion, of trial and error, and a time of learning and self-discovery begin. That which is universally wise now becomes individually aware and therefore limited. The general becomes the particular. The macrocosm becomes the microcosm.

The whorls on the child's finger tips will mark him as a distinctive individual, and traits of personality and character will endear him to others. But all that distinguishes him also disguises him, for no description can describe the Indescribable and no name or mark can define the Ineffable. "Why," said the angel to the father of Samson, "askest thou thus after my name, seeing it is secret?" (Judges 13:18) And God bade Moses to hide himself in the cleft of the rock "while my glory passeth by . . . thou shalt see my back parts but my face shall not be seen." (Ex. 33:22-23) The whole phenomenal world is the back or visible part of the noumenal world, or God. Every new-born child is a re-presentation of the One.

The little one comes to us as "ours." But he is not "ours." We never owned him. What we never owned, we can never lose. As Gibran observes, he came through us but not by us. Parents are only the mediums of manifestation. You never did possess what you have not now lost. If the meaning of every human life is the coming and going of the Infinite, then that meaning is forever, and with clearer seeing nothing will be lost to our now sense-clouded mind. As hundreds before have observed, birth and death are doors.

Belief in immortality helps. For then one cannot grieve, knowing that his beloved has gone a little way ahead on a journey which we will all take. What we have once known we shall meet again, every longing of the heart fulfilled, every basic instinct satisfied. But even without this conviction, many will agree that death is a release from body sickness or crystallization of mind. Let us go back to the little child in order to see how this happens. The little child comes into this life, buoyant and eager, all of his senses hungry for experience. Then as he "grows older" the senses withdraw and his spirit gets broken or badly bent; his outlook narrows, egotism governs him and like a machine he goes on repeating, neither learning nor growing. Manly Hall (Death and After, Philosopher's Press, Los Angeles) observes that "There is a period in everyone's life where mentally and spiritually he dies and after that the sooner physical death follows the better." Mr. Hall once stood watching a slow-moving, mud-covered water buffalo dragging a primitive plow through the ooze of a partly submerged rice field. Hour after hour the animal labored, shaking its massive head to free it of swarms of flies. Behind the bull walked an aged man, his tattered trousers rolled above his knees and bespattered with ooze and grime. To wade day after wearisome day through the rice paddies constituted the life of the bull. To follow with hands on the plow constituted the life of the man. Is it a blessing to prolong the life of these two beyond a certain point where they can learn anything new? "Suppose," says Mr. Hall, "that instead of living threescore years and ten, the gray-haired man had to live a thousand years! Would he not plow the mud of the rice fields day after day? What would he know after a thousand years that he did not already know?"

We die when our work is done, when the spirit no longer inquires, when the future no longer beckons, when every changing scene repeats the meaning of the previous one, when either by losing the inclination to learn anything new or by having made the most of our talents and opportunities, life here holds no further challenge or invitation to our powers.

All of this helps us to accept the fact of death, not as unmixed tragedy, but as a meaningful experience in and of life. Since death has cosmic significance, it cannot have personal harm. As facts and playwrights have portrayed it, death comes as a friend. Most people who are conscious just before death declare that they are better. Apparently, no one looked into the face of death and found it terrifying. There was kindness there. For centuries, observers of the dying have noted that at that moment when the soul knows death is inevitable, "the subjective mind (soul) takes complete possession, the objective senses are benumbed, the body is anesthetized, and the patient dies, without pain and without regret." (Thomas J. Hudson, Law of Psychic Phenomena, McClurg 1900)

Twice in our lives, our judgments of others are pure—one is the time we first fall in love, the other is time of death. To the lover, all is beautiful and lovely with the beloved. Every limitation is hidden in a golden mist. This beautiful feature is also in death. The small faults of the one we loved are carried away. Professor Mueller observed, "We always judge in self-defense and that makes our judgments so harsh." When others are gone, how readily we forgive, how truly we love! When the matter is taken from our hands and the Beneficence of Life takes over, then we are at our best in judgment and in love. There is no evil where love is lord of all.

Death is hard but death is also kind. It is the one thing which reduces our inflated egotism and modifies our false pride. Death opens our eyes to what is beyond the senses. It is a doorway to greater life for both deceased and survivor. Were one daily to reckon more with death while still alive, we should not be so unprepared, we should be able to address death as friend, we should know that we are spirits first and bodies second, with discerning minds somewhere between. Bodies are instruments which we use like garments, discarding the old for a new one. That of us which was not born, cannot cease to be. Life is a ceaseless progression through worlds that are infinite. Bodies are things of time and space. They can be separated by time and by space. Spirits are outside time and space. They are everywhere and anywhere. Whenever we think of each other, we are together. Whatever we have known and whatever has known us, is ours still. Love is the union of spirits which do not decay and are inseparable. As a dying wife said to her husband, "Go on with your work; I shall help you 'there' as I have done 'here.' Only do not call upon me unless you really need me, for I shall have my own work to do."

CHRISTIAN SCIENCE AND DEATH

Robert Peel

It is remarkable that the most compassionate of men is credited with a statement which many people might regard as a cruelly delusive promise: "Whosoever liveth and believeth in me shall never die" (John 11:26). Christian Scientists find it essential to grasp the concept of life and death which these words imply.

Regarded as a finite, material process, life is clearly doomed to end in death. Even the potentially indefinite preservation of a living organism by biochemical means is confronted by the fact that the solar system itself must eventually perish. Matter holds no promise of immortality.

The life of Jesus Christ, however, stands in stark contrast to this picture of unrelieved mortality. His resurrection, as the New Testament presents it and as primitive Christianity accepted it, is the symbol and guarantee of a continuity of individual consciousness beyond the grave. Christian Science goes one step further and states that Christ's later "ascension" beyond all material conditions is evidence that man's essential being is wholly spiritual.

To the Christian Scientist, Life *is* Spirit, and Spirit is God, the creative Love from which man draws his individual being. Holding to this conviction, it is impossible to regard death as more than a phase, however grievous it may seem, of mankind's imperfect sense of life. It is as though a friend we love has gone to a distant country and is physically unable to communicate with those he left behind, but in the new country he finds renewed opportunities for meaningful progress and self-fulfillment.

This view of death differs markedly from the traditional concept of a heavenly hereafter. It demands an understanding of reality as the inner spiritual dimension of experience—the true substance at which the life of the senses can only hint. The Christian Scientist believes that we awaken to this reality, both here and hereafter, not through dying but through living, not through the annihilation of individuality but through a deepening awareness of identity as rooted in spiritual being.

67

To all but the doctrinaire materialist, a person one has loved is not a body composed of physical atoms; he is the individualized qualities of mind, heart, and spirit intimately known by us in concrete experience. As we penetrate deeper into the heart of reality, nothing can keep us from appreciating these qualities more profoundly and incorporating them more creatively in our own lives. In this sense, rather than in a psychic or spiritistic sense, we can even come to know better the true identity of those whom we have lost physically.

A Christian Scientist, confronted with death, ponders these things not as philosophic abstractions but as living truths. The result is often a sudden or rapid healing of grief—even an upswelling of joy and courage to go forward, although sometimes the struggle may be long and severe. Occasionally a Christian Scientist may mistakenly feel that he must hide grief with a patently false cheerfulness, but a deeper realism can bring the kind of insight that enabled Paul to write, "Death is swallowed up in victory" (I Cor. 15:54).

Again, if the loved one has died while undergoing Science treatment, there may be great dismay that an expected healing failed to materialize. Experience has taught Christian Scientists that even the most extreme case of organic disease is not beyond God's healing power. In fact, there are even cases on record where healings have occurred after death had apparently taken place. (See *A Century of Christian Science Healing*: Boston, 1966). But Christian Scientists know that they still have a long way to go before they can always attain the unfailing certainty of Jesus' healing.

However, they can take further comfort in the words of Paul that the last enemy to be destroyed is death. The founder of Christian Science, Mary Baker Eddy, pointed out that immense time and spiritual growth are required before we can triumph completely over the last enemy. She wrote in *Unity of Good* (p. 40), "To say that you and I, as mortals, will not enter this dark shadow of material sense, called *death*, is to assert what we have not proved." But she went on to draw a clear-cut distinction between our present limited perception of life and the continuity of real being. Man in his true being, according to this interpretation, can never die.

This distinction takes us further into the metaphysics of Christian Science than is appropriate in so brief a sketch as the present one, but it serves as a reminder that Christian Scientists place all temporal events within a frame of reference which radically transforms the values of these events. The acknowledgment of God as all-encompassing Life and Love does not lead to the ascetic otherworldliness of medieval Christianity with its virtual worship of death but to a vastly enlarged concept of living.

This view influences such matters as burial and funerals. There is no general rule or pattern concerning these practices; some Christian Scientists may choose interment in a family plot, others cremation. In either case, the bodily remains are not in themselves an object of veneration. The individual, Christian Science teaches, is more than the body with which we identify him; as Mrs. Eddy wrote in her major work, *Science and Health with Key to the Scriptures* (p. 429), "Mortals waken from the dream of death with bodies unseen by those who think that they bury the body."

Funeral services may be held at home or in a funeral parlor. Some families prefer not to have them at all; others (probably the majority) have a simple memorial service, consisting chiefly of readings from the Bible and Mrs. Eddy's writings. In the service the emphasis is on life, rather than death. The family and friends of the departed are reminded that he can never be separated from the Life that is God. To him, as to those present, the Psalmist's words apply: "I shall not die, but live, and declare the works of the Lord" (Ps. 118:17). It is not unusual for healings of grief to take place at these services.

Often a bereaved person may turn to a Christian Science practitioner for help in finding his bearings in the new situation confronting him. Ordinarily a practitioner does not attempt to direct his actions or give him what Christian Scientists refer to as "human advice." The practitioner's primary task is to awaken him more fully to God's presence, power, and guidance—to turn his thoughts to the divine Mind, which knows and supplies his needs more effectively than any finite counselor could do.

Christians and humanists alike regard human life as a learning process in which we may ultimately gain from our losses and mistakes.

Christian Scientists understand that the real meaning of this education is the discovery and demonstration of our common life in God. In *Science and Health* (p. 322) we find: "The sharp experiences of belief in the supposititious life of matter, as well as our disappointments and ceaseless woes, turn us like tired children to the arms of divine Love. Then we begin to learn Life in divine Science."

Estrangement from divine Life is the basis of all finitude, all loss and separation. Healing begins as we accept that deathless Life as our own.

REFERENCES TO LIFE AND DEATH, TRIBUTE AND MEMORY: *THE OLD TESTAMENT*

Selected by SIDNEY NATHANSON

There is but one step between me and death. Samuel 1,20:3

Lord make me to know mine end, and the measure of my days, what it is; let me know how short-lived I am. Psalms 39:5

We bring our years to an end as a tale that is told. Psalms 90:9

The days of our years are three score years or even by reason of strength fourscore years, yet is their pride but travail and vanity for it is speedily gone and we fly away. Psalms 90:10

Man is born unto trouble, as the sparks fly upward. Job 5:7

Our days upon the earth are like a shadow. Job 8:9

To everything there is a season, and a time to every purpose under the heaven: a time to be born, and a time to die. Ecclesiastes 3:1cf

I shall go to him, but he shall not return to me. Samuel II, 12:23

I go the way of all the earth: be thou strong therefore and show thyself a man. Kings I, 2:2

Set thine house in order; for thus shalt die, and not live. Kings II, 20:1

If a man live many years, let him rejoice in them all; and remember the days of darkness; for they shall be many. Ecclesiastes 11:8

He will swallow up death forever, and the Lord God will wipe away tears from off all faces. Isaiah 25:8

Comfort ye, comfort ye, my people, saith your God. Isaiah 40:1

Thy sun shall no more go down, neither shall thy moon withdraw itself: for the Lord shall be thine everlasting light, and the days of thy mourning shall be ended. Isaiah 60:20

For thou wilt not abandon my soul to the netherworld; neither wilt thou suffer thy godly one to see the pit. Psalms 16:10

Into thine hand I commit my spirit; thou hast redeemed me, O Lord, thou God of truth.   Psalms 31:5

Mark the man of integrity and behold the upright: for there is a future for the man of peace.   Psalms 37:37

He will cover thee with his pinions and under His wings shalt thou take refuge; His truth is a shield and a buckler.   Psalms 91:4

He will give His angels charge over thee, to keep thee in all thy ways.
                                                        Psalms 91:11

A good man leaveth an inheritance to his children's children.
                                                    Proverbs 13:22

Righteousness delivereth from death.   Proverbs 10:2

The Lord shall keep thee from all evil: he shall keep thy soul. The Lord shall guard thy going out and thy coming in from this time forth and forever.   Psalms 121:7,8

Surely there is a future and thy hope wilt not be cut off.
                                                    Proverbs 23:18

Her children rise up and call her blessed, her husband also, and he praiseth her.   Proverbs 31:28

The spirit of man is the lamp of the Lord, searching all the inward parts.   Proverbs 20:27

Till I die I will not put away mine integrity from me.   Job 27:5

One generation passeth away, and another generation cometh: and the earth abideth forever.   Ecclesiastes 1:4

Remember also thy creator in the days of thy youth, or ever the evil days come and the years draw nigh, when thou shalt say, I have no pleasure in them; or ever the sun and the light, and the moon, and the stars be darkened and the clouds return after the rain: and the dust return to the Earth as it was: and the spirit to God who gave it. This is the end of the matter; all hath been heard: fear God and His commandments, for this is the whole duty of man.
                                            Ecclesiastes 12:1,2,7,13

The righteous are even greater in death than in life.   Talmud

Men may be compared to the grass of the field—both sprout up and both wither away. Talmud

This world is but a stop-over place. Midrash

Why dost thou pride thyself with a world that is not thine own? Talmud

The world is like a vestibule before the world to come: prepare thyself in the vestibule that thou mayest enter the hall. Talmud

Would that life were like the shadow cast by a wall or a tree; but it is like the shadow of a bird in flight. Midrash

The righteous even after their death are called alive. Talmud

The wicked even while alive are called dead. Talmud

Whoever weeps over a worthy person has all his sins forgiven because of the honor shown the deceased. Talmud

The tears which are shed over a worthy person, God places in his treasure-house. Talmud

The soul of a man mourns over him the first seven days after his death. Talmud

When the righteous passes away the loss is sustained by his whole generation. Talmud

There are some who die before their time. Talmud

Some win eternal life only after many years, others, a single hour. Talmud

Do not comfort thy fellow in the hour that his dead lies before him. Talmud

They that are born are destined to die, and the dead to be brought to life again. Talmud

In the hour of man's departure neither silver nor gold nor precious stones nor pearls accompany him, but only the Torah and good deeds. Talmud

When man is born into this world, his hands are clenched tightly as if to say, 'The entire world is mine, even my possessions.' When he departs from the world, his palms are open, as if to say, 'I have taken nothing away with me from this world.'   Midrash

In the day of death a man considers that he has lived but a single day.
                                                                    Zohar

The righteous need no memorials, their words and deeds are their remembrances.   Talmud

REFERENCES TO DEATH AND BEREAVEMENT:
THE NEW TESTAMENT

Selected by WALTER DEBOLD

Jesus said: I am the resurrection. If anyone believes in me, even though he dies he will live, and whoever lives and believes in me will never die. John: 11,26

But we believe that having died with Christ we shall return to life with him: Christ, as we know, having been raised from the dead will never die again. Death has no power over him any more. When he died, he died, once for all, to sin, so his life now is life with God; and in that way, you too must consider yourselves to be dead to sin but alive for God in Christ Jesus. Romans: 6,8-11

If we have died with him, then we shall live with him.
If we hold firm, then we shall reign with him.
If we disown him, then he will disown us.
We may be unfaithful, but he is always faithful,
for he cannot disown his own self. 2 Timothy: 2,12-13

But Christ has in fact been raised from the dead, the first fruits of all who have fallen asleep. 1 Corinthians: 15,20

Happy are those who die in the Lord! Happy indeed, the Spirit says; now they can rest for ever after their work, since their good deeds go with them. Revelations: 14,13

God would not be so unjust as to forget all you have done.
Hebrews: 6,10

I have told you all this so that you may find peace in me.
John: 16,33

The love of Christ overwhelms us. 2 Corinthians: 5,14

When we were baptized in Christ Jesus we were baptized in his death.
Romans: 6,3

If in union with Christ we have imitated his death, we shall also imitate him in his resurrection. Romans: 6,5

75

But when Christ is revealed—and he is your life—you too will be revealed in all your glory with him.   Colossians: 3,4

Christ suffered for you and left an example for you to follow the way he took.   1 Peter: 2,21

If by the Spirit you put an end to the misdeeds of the body you will live.   Romans: 8,13

We carry with us in our body the death of Jesus, so that the life of Jesus, too, may always be seen in our bodies.   2 Corinthians: 4,10

All I want is to know Christ and the power of his resurrection and to share his sufferings by reproducing the pattern of his death.
Philippians: 3,10

The life and death of each of us has its influence on others; if we live, we live for the Lord; and if we die, we die for the Lord, so that alive or dead we belong to the Lord.   Romans: 14, 7-8

Life to me, of course, is Christ, but then death would bring me something more.   Philippians: 1,21

And then, if my blood has to be shed as part of your own sacrifice and offering—which is your faith—I shall still be happy and rejoice with all of you, and you must be just as happy and rejoice with me.
Philippians: 2, 17-18

We want you to be quite certain, brothers, about those who have died, to make sure that you do not grieve about them, like the other people who have no hope.   1 Thessalonians: 4,11

Joseph of Arimathaea . . . boldly went to Pilate and asked for the body of Jesus.   Mark: 15,43

Just as all men die in Adam, so all men will be brought to life in Christ.   1 Corinthians: 15,22

There will be no more death and no more mourning or sadness.
Revelations: 21,4

Death is swallowed up in victory. Death where is your victory? Death where is your sting?   1 Corinthians: 16,55

As one man's fall brought condemnation on everyone, so the good act of one man brings everyone life and makes them justified.

Romans: 5,18

For the wage paid by sin is death; the present given by God is eternal life in Christ Jesus our Lord.

Romans: 6,23

REFERENCES TO DEATH AND BEREAVEMENT:
THE OLD TESTAMENT

He will destroy death forever.	Isaiah: 25,8
Where is your plague, Death?	Hosea: 13,14
Do not neglect to honour his grave.	Ecclesiasticus: 38,16
Let grief end with the funeral.	Ecclesiasticus: 38,19
Do not abandon your heart to grief.	Ecclesiasticus: 38,20

TO THE PARENT

Park J. White

"A voice is heard in Ramah,—lamentation and bitter weeping: Rachel weeping for her children refuses to be comforted, because they are not."   (Jeremiah: 31, 15; Matthew: 2, 18)

Parental grief was as poignant, as apparently insusceptible of comfort in Rachel's time, 3,600 years ago, as it is today. Many grief-stricken parents seem to reject consolation that may, at times be clumsily proffered; but few indeed are they who intend to act that way. People may obtain relief by taking it out on someone else, whether it be the sympathizer or even God who gave and who now takes away the life of a loved one.

Fortunate are the bereaved who are in close association with relatives, ministers, doctors, or teachers who are gifted with the fine art of giving sympathy. Knowing that some can express proper feelings better than others, St. Paul wrote to the Romans, "Rejoice with them that do rejoice, mourn with them that weep." It is quite possible to be helpful, come weal, come woe.

Sympathy, walking with friend or relative through the valley of the shadow, must come naturally; and the mourner should accept it with grace. It must be given to the sympathizer in that hour what he shall say—or whether he shall say anything at all. At the same time the bereaved should share his own troubled thoughts with those who are willing to listen.

O timeless Scripture! Rachel mourning her children in Ramah and twentieth-century parents laid low by the same misfortune are indeed in similar situations. But the scene and the principals are so very, very different, mainly because of the ascendancy of science and the scientific approach. Jesus said, "Ye shall know the truth, and the truth shall make you free."

The scientific person does not require all the answers. At any rate, in his search for the truth, he does not get them. He knows, and should even be consoled by the fact, that his job is to seek these answers with all his might. But even as we toil together, we are blessed if we can say, as Jesus had to say in Gethsemane, "Not as I will, but as Thou wilt." For us, consolation can be found in study and action, plus as much faith as we can muster.

And so we consider again infant mortality from the point of view of trying to keep Rachel from having to weep for her children. We men, God's instruments, must admit that from the beginning of recorded time until this century, we have scarcely made a dent in the infant mortality rates. God's timing is so hard—nay, impossible—to explain! The long delay in the coming of our knowledge of bacteriology, sanitation, preventive medicine, has dotted the graveyards with tiny graves. Poor Rachels!

No doctor ever gives up trying to save a child-patient. The resilience of children, even with death obviously close, is phenomenal. True, a resurgence of health and humor may be only a temporary remission; but even this is welcomed by the patient and his team. Also, might not this respite be just long enough to enable the doctors to take advantage of the long-hoped-for breakthrough discovery? Remember the advent of insulin, the sulfas, penicillin, streptomycin?

No parents can accept without pain the prospect of early death for a child who is hopelessly ill. But those closest to the young patient may derive at least a little solace from what remaining time is given them to help; as they summon up all their spiritual and all their emotional control, they can share with dignity the child's final days.

To the Parent

PRAYER CAN HELP

Belief in a Supreme Being need not rob people of their intellectual values. Prayer is not synonymous with a blind demand for comfort in the shape of miracles. It is true that our desperation over the impending death of a beloved child may drive us to arrogant, demanding prayer. But we should know better than to pray—or rather, to command—as Moses did when his sister Miriam was stricken with leprosy, "Heal her *now*, O Lord!"

If we walk humbly, if our soul's sincere desire, uttered or unexpressed, is humble rather than demanding, our prayer should echo that of blind, undemanding George Croly:

We ask no dream, no prophet-ecstasies,
No sudden rending of the veil of clay,
No angel-visitant, no opening skies;
But take the dimness of our souls away.

Teach us to feel that thou art always nigh;
Teach us the struggles of the souls to bear,
To check the rising doubt, the rebel sigh;
Teach us the patience of unanswered prayer.

We cannot aver that either science or religion can answer all our needs. But they that mourn may yet realize that there does exist a Universal Love; that in it they are blessed; and thus they may be comforted.

C. DYING

THE RIGHT TO DIE

MARVIN GOLDFINE

We are each given life. We did not choose it, unless each day's persistence in life is taken as a form of choosing. Whence, then, our right to abrogate it? Does suffering or pain confer it? Despair, ennui, a sense of emptiness, disappointment—do these confer it? In the latter cases, we might understand and sympathize, but rarely would we go so far as to agree that these grant the right. We would try to treat, to help, to encourage—and when such an approach failed, we would make every effort to forestall and prevent the ultimate calamity. Rarely do we affirm the patient's right to pursue his tragic purpose. Is physical suffering in a different category?

If the patient cannot bring himself to such an act, may others step in and determine this for him? Even with his declared request and consent? And when should such a right be exercised for him? When his condition reaches a stage bordering on terminus? Assuming this to be determinable—and it is quite questionable—who gives the go-ahead sign? The spouse? The children? Others? Can we always be sure that motives are absolutely pure and selfless? How do we separate our own pain and grief as onlookers from that of the patient as sufferer?

To place the burden of decision and commission on the physician, even if he were to accept it, holds dangers and complications that should give us pause in affirming such a right. Every physician will testify to his over-riding obligation to cherish and preserve life. True, there are undeniable situations wherein the end seems certain, wherein experience leaves little room for doubt about the outcome, and in which the material and psychological drain on families is incalculable. In such cases, some physicians will not hesitate to allow death to take its course for the sake of the mental health of survivors. Others would resist even in such contingencies, both on grounds of principle as well as the more practical considerations of how and where to draw the line between the clear-cut and the less clear-cut situation. Human destiny, by its very nature, knows of no certainties so long as life pulsates within the body.

The right to die—before one's time—is a "right" that has very limited public recognition. It is still considered illegal to exercise it, and, by many, morally reprehensible to condone it. There are special groups and scattered individuals who voice strong objection to the prevailing practice and attitude, but it is an issue that is still unresolved and is likely to remain so for years to come.

THE HOSPITAL CHAPLAIN LOOKS AT DEATH
IN A RESEARCH SETTING

LeRoy G. Kerney

It was a scene I shall never forget. Mr. Fowler had said "good-by" to his wife for the last time. She had been a patient in a medical research hospital. They had been a devoted couple. With their children grown and out of the home, they were particularly close as husband and wife. Now in their early seventies, they had lived full and meaningful lives.

He had brought her to the research hospital with the hope that medical answers could be found that were not available in his home community. He had urged her to become a patient there in order to keep alive the hopes and dreams they shared. New medical procedures and drugs had been tried. For a while her condition improved; then it changed rapidly. Early in the evening, doctors and technicians scurried around her bed in a valiant attempt to keep her alive. Strange machines and equipment were moved in. Unfamiliar faces hovered over her. But in a short while it was over.

The doctor left the room and walked down the corridor to Mr. Fowler. He told him that they had tried their best but the best was not enough. They were sorry. As they went into the doctor's office, the doctor asked Mr. Fowler for permission to perform an autopsy. Quietly, he signed the consent form. An administrative aide appeared to discuss the funeral arrangements with him. Did he know of a funeral home in his community that he would like to have handle the arrangements? He was asked to sign for his wife's clothes and belongings.

As the chaplain on call, I had come to the hospital to see Mr. Fowler. After greeting him, I asked him a few simple questions about his wife. With an occasional tear in his eye, he shared briefly a few of his memories of their life together. Our conversation concluded with a prayer. "Dear God, we thank thee for the life of Mrs. Fowler, for the life she shared with her husband, and the contribution she has made to medical research. Give Mr. Fowler the strength to walk confidently through the valley of the shadows and give him comfort and meaning in the days to come. Amen."

A nursing aide carried the clothes and the few belongings to Mr. Fowler's car. As we stepped through the door of the hospital, we walked into a dark and lonely world. It was midnight; the air was cold but still. We walked to the car in silence. When we came to the car, he stopped, thanked me, shook my hand, and then drove off. The picture of this lonely man, with his wife's pocket-book hung over his arm as he walked into the night, is a scene that is etched indelibly in my memory.

Although this memory is a poignant and vivid one for me, it is not unique. Others, like Mr. Fowler, having just lost a loved one, have been left behind in a lonely world. What is unique is the setting in which grief was experienced. In this case, it was a medical research hospital. How does the medical research setting affect the grief experience? In what way do the factors peculiar to such a setting influence and condition the meaning of grief for the bereaved? These are the questions we wish to explore.

Although he knew the pain of grief actually, Mr. Fowler, like most individuals, probably was not acquainted with many of the details of medical research. What is medical research? What impact has it had on our lives? How is it regulated and controlled?

In medical research, procedures may be included which are not generally accepted as being for the direct therapeutic benefit of a patent or as an aid in the diagnosis of his disease. These often consist of the use of new techniques or drugs that have been developed in medical laboratories and appear to have promise in the treatment and diagnosis of an illness.

Medical research has created a quiet revolution in the practice of medicine. Tremendous strides have been made in the understanding of biological processes and in the medical profession's ability to treat many diseases. Thanks to the advent of antibiotics, new surgical techniques and drugs, many persons have survived who a few decades ago would have succumbed to their illness. The American Medical Association recently reported that seven out of ten products on the market now were not available ten years ago. Modern knowledge has changed the approach to the treatment of diseases and has given new hope and life.

However, medical research carries with it two kinds of risks. If nothing is attempted, nothing is gained. At the same time, if the risks that are taken are not calculated, carefully regulated, and controlled, a waste of human suffering, if not life, can result. Much time, effort, and thought has been and is being given to establishing guidelines and creating structures to regulate medical research. The main principles guiding clinical research are: (1) group consideration, including evaluation of peer judgment on the part of the investigating team; (2) informed consent by the patient or normal (control) subject participation in such a project; and (3) the right of the patient or normal volunteer to withdraw from the research project at any time. These basic principles were formulated in 1949 in the judgments of the Trials of War Criminals by the Nuremberg Military Tribunal for "The Medical Case." Since then, these policies have been and are being greatly refined and further articulated in order to protect individuals participating in such studies. Overriding caution and agonizing concern are given by administrators and investigators in approving and conducting medical research.

Grief in a medical research setting is affected by the hopes and expectations of the patients and their families. Many patients are referred to medical research programs after "established" means and methods of medical treatment have proved inadequate in the treatment of their specific illness. Mr. Fowler brought his wife to the research hospital in the hope that medical answers could be found that were not available in his home community. Acceptance for treatment in a medical research program often revives the hopes for relief or cure and keeps alive the human expectations that positive answers will be found for puzzling problems. Usually these hopes and expectations are appropriate and realistic.

Mr. Fowler's expectations were quite realistic. He knew his wife had a life-threatening illness. He knew that unless something different were done for his wife, she could not continue to live. Having been accepted for participation in a research study, the Fowlers came to the hospital with realistic hope. Mr. Fowler wanted his wife to have the opportunity to receive investigational drugs in the hope of

89

prolonging her life. With sadness in his heart, he evinced the quiet grief that appears in an older, mature person who has shared his life with another individual in a meaningful way. But his grief was not compounded by disappointment. He had faced the possibility that she might not survive. They had shared this with each other several times during her last days. The blow was softened by his realization that he had tried to do all that could possibly be done for her. Knowing this did not restore her to life, but it did help him feel that he had been faithful to her to the end.

In contrast, the Smiths brought Ann, their six-year-old girl, for treatment of a congenital heart defect. The doctors told them about a new surgical procedure that had real promise. Since it had been tried on only a limited number of cases, it offered both risk as well as hope. They had focused on the hopes and repressed the negative possibilities, despite the fact that they had been informed in detail of the range of possible outcomes to the operation. Ann died two days after surgery. Disappointed and shocked, the parents were swamped with grief. Their grief, experienced in a medical research setting, was affected by the hopes and expectations they had been given by a new medical discovery.

In a medical research setting, personal involvement in decision-making also leads to grief that is compounded with feelings of guilt —since participation is on a voluntary basis and the final decision is made by the patient, usually in consultation with his family. Relatives feel an involvement in and, in some measure, responsibility for the outcome because they have been drawn into the decision-making process.

Ann's parents felt at the time of her death that if they had not chosen to bring their daughter to the research hospital, she might have lived a few more years. They felt responsible for the decision to proceed with the operation; and they felt a strong sense of guilt over their daughter's death. Their grief was compounded with feelings of guilt over the decision to which they had been a party.

John was a 17-year-old patient who came to the research hospital with his parents. Examination confirmed that a growth in his leg was malignant, and surgery was recommended as the treatment of choice.

The doctors shared their findings with the patient and his family. They pointed out that they would not know the extent of the growth or how much tissue would have to be removed until they operated. John and his parents signed the consent form. During surgery, it was discovered that the malignancy was much more extensive than had been anticipated. The patient's leg had to be amputated to make sure that no cancer cells had been left. When the mother was told of the extent of the surgery, she became shocked and dazed. As she began to translate her feelings and experiences into words, she angrily said to me, "The doctor did not tell me John might lose his entire leg." I knew that she had been told the full story, but had not heard what she had not wished to hear. In her shocked condition she said, "I would just as soon he were dead." Although the boy made a fine recovery, I am sure that had he died, the mother would have been overwhelmed with guilt because she had been a part of the consent process.

Sometimes the feelings of guilt arise because the new procedures or drugs seem to exact too high a price in suffering, misery, and pain. Grief seems not to have occurred because the relative could not find available a course that would promise to extend life; rather, he suffered from the feeling of guilt that accompanies grief over having permitted the loved one to be subjected to well-intended but futile medical means.

Grief in a medical research setting is often experienced as grief among strangers and the unfamiliar. To move to a medical research setting means to be involved with new and unfamiliar faces, names, procedures, equipment, and routines.

Let us return to our story of Mr. Fowler, by himself, the night his wife died. He was too far from home to be visited by an occasional friend, relative, or neighbor. During his wife's hospitalization, his clergyman had visited once but could not come regularly. His children, who were married and lived a considerable distance away, talked to him often by phone; but they were not available to stand by him at the time of death. Those in the hospital tried to reach out to him in his grief. The doctor tried to convey his sympathy. The nurses expressed their appreciation for the kindness and consideration Mrs. Fowler had given them during her stay in the hospital. The chaplain endeavored to express the concern of the religious community for her loss and shared with him familiar words and religious symbols that would give support and meaning in his time of bereavement.

Mr. Fowler had left his family, friends, and neighbors to find a new community of persons at the hospital. When his wife died, he left these new-found friends to return home. As a chaplain, I was aware that though my ministry hopefully would be helpful to him in the hospital, I would not be the clergyman who would conduct the funeral services for his wife. Nor would I be able to minister to him during the weeks that would follow the funeral. His children did not have the opportunity to visit their mother during her last days and to know first-hand her courage, faith, and love. Their grief could not be the same as it would have been had they been able to participate in those last painful but meaningful moments.

There are powerful positive factors that also affect grief in a medical research setting. Such grief may be accompanied by a sense of purpose that comes from participation in medical research. On the back of the worship folder used in the Protestant Chapel services at the Clinical Center of the National Institutes of Health, Bethesda, Maryland, is found the following words:

> "Offering is our response to God in worship. We respond to God with our sacrifices of praise and thanksgiving, in offering ourselves in His service, and in bearing each other's burdens. Our contributions to the research programs of this hospital can be understood as an offering to God. We pray God will transform our suffering into meaningful knowledge that will prevent disease, alleviate suffering, and prolong life. Seen in this light, the significance of our suffering is beyond comprehension."

As a chaplain, I often point out to grieving families that perhaps the final part that has been played by the person who has just died is a piece of a medical jig-saw puzzle that in time will be fitted in with other fragments of knowledge to create new patterns of treatment and cure. The grieving person may finally know that the suffering and death of the loved one is not all lost and wasted.

Sometimes reluctance to grant permission for an autopsy is caused by failure to understand the importance of a postmortem medical examination. Mrs. Jones, a young bride of only two months, came to a research hospital with a life-threatening disease. After a few days in the hospital she died quite unexpectedly. The doctors had known her prognosis was very poor but were puzzled by the suddenness of her expiration. The husband refused to grant permission for an autopsy until he could discuss it with his mother-in-law. She arrived a half hour later. After a conference with the doctor on duty, she, too, refused to consent to a postmortem. As the chaplain who had been called to the hospital, I talked with both the husband and his mother-in-law. I discovered that the mother-in-law had refused because she was confident that the correct diagnosis had been established and could see no need for an autopsy. It was explained to her that although the diagnosis was probably correct, an autopsy could answer many more commanding practical as well as research questions. Then she gave her consent readily.

Sometimes the withholding of permission for autopsy is an expression of the family's hostility toward a doctor. Occasionally, the refusal is based on religious grounds. A Jewish chaplain told me about a man who instructed his family to grant permission for an autopsy to be performed on his body despite the fact that it was against their religious beliefs, as they understood them. The patient had said, "I don't want my suffering to go to waste." This is the basic reason for consenting to an autopsy. The bereaved can look back on the loss and find positive meaning in the midst of their grief experience.

In summary, the experience of grief and its meaning is affected and influenced by the medical research setting. It is affected by the hopes and expectations that patients and their families place in clinical research programs, and by participation in the decision-making process that sometimes leads to feelings of guilt. It is influenced by the unfamiliar nature of the setting and the involvement with strangers. It is also conditioned by the sense of purpose and meaning that comes from participation in a medical research program.

Awareness of these factors and the effect they have on grief is most important in dealing with the loss of a loved one.

Although the focus of concern of the above discussion is the medical research setting, factors found in that particular environment are implicit if not explicit in all medical settings. It is also our belief that with the changes in medical care and health programs these factors will become increasingly prominent in all medical settings and, therefore, will affect the experience of grief similarly.

The Editors

AUTOPSY PERMISSION

Marvin Goldfine

Before he has a chance to emerge from the initial shock of a loved one's death and its immediate effects, the principal survivor may be approached by the doctor about the need for an autopsy. Whatever course he chooses, it would be best for him first to follow studiously the considerations involved as presented by the doctor. Too often the mind is closed on the subject before all the factors are made known. Some people react unequivocally and with emotional horror against any thought of mutilating the body of a dear one. Some go to the other extreme of assuming that every suggestion along such lines by the doctor constitutes an irresistible call to come to the aid of science.

What is demanded in facing the question is an ability and willingness to weigh carefully such variables as the nature and extent of the medical problem with which the examination purports to deal, the extent of the mutilation involved, the religious factor, if any, and the wishes of the deceased, if known to the survivor.

Of the three major faiths in the United States, only traditional Judaism looks with disfavor on the dissection of the human body. Its position is based on the principle that no deceased body—not even that of a condemned criminal—may be treated with the slightest disrespect, a view derived from Deuteronomy 21.23, which enjoins burial of one condemned to death by hanging on the same day. However, there are exceptional situations in which this principle is set aside, as when there is an immediate prospect of saving life from the knowledge thus gained, or to establish whether a murder had been committed.

In general, only one in complete possession of himself can deal with the question fairly. Since such detachment is not usual so soon after the moment of death, advice should be sought from friends or counselors—possibly a clergyman or lawyer—who could be helpful.

SUSPENDED DEATH

Edgar N. Jackson

Man's overwhelming fear of death can lead him to think irrational thoughts and do unwisely considered deeds.

Many persons have been cruelly victimized by fake mediums who have claimed to restore communication with the dead. Although we would not deny the possibility that some portions of the human personality survive the biological event of death, abuses by the fraudulent spiritualist is a simple fact that indicates man's susceptibility to the fear of death and his need to guarantee the projection of his own life into an eternal dimension.

Each age has its own way of coping with this fear of death. In a scientific age, it is not strange that we should see some of the advancements in physics and chemistry employed to produce the same effects. Scientific claims of possible means to stay the processes of bodily disintegration, with the hope that at some future date the advancements in medicine could in some way find means of overcoming the cause of death, is a modern variation on an old theme.

Our preoccupation with the apprehension about death and the distressing emotions that go with acute grief may make us vulnerable to such schemes. To restore some measure of objectivity, it may be wise for us to consider the economic, social, and spiritual aspects of these suggested procedures.

Physical death is considered to be a biological event, but it is also recognized as a legal fact, changing the status of relationship of the persons involved. It touches matters of marriage, property, personal possessions, and legal relationships in partnerships and corporate ventures. To create a state of uncertain death would project uncertainty and confusion into an endless number of human and economic relationships.

Basically, all religions have been concerned with building a sound philosophy of life and death to help men cope with the spiritual nature of man in relation to the physical event we call death. It is claimed by the Christian faith that a man does not begin to reach the full measure of his spiritual existence until he can "taste of death." We are taught that "like a grain of wheat" we must fall to the earth in order to go through the metamorphosis that produces new life. To violate this basic tenet of faith would be to make many of the assumptions of that faith irrelevant for the living of life.

The hazard of this effort to create a suspended state of death is the projection of the anxiety of a death-denying, death-defying cultural climate in many directions, and there is no telling what the ultimate outcome may be. It makes the assumption that the process of nature with its orderly progression of life and death is basically unsound, and that man in his practice of applied science can outwit the basic order of nature. It is quite a different thing from the skill of the physician who prolongs life by his conquest of disease, to prolong death in the vain hope that at some future date life can be restored. It could well be one of the most cruel acts of victimizing human anxiety to extract large amounts of money from people on a shallow promise that has neither proven scientific backing nor adequate philosophical premise.

TO DISCUSS ARRANGEMENTS OR NOT

ROBERT B. REEVES, JR.

One day I got an urgent phone call from a nurse, saying that the doctor wanted me to see a patient who was "morbidly obsessed" with the thought of dying. When I heard the patient's name, I was somewhat surprised, for this was someone I knew: a woman who had been in the hospital several times before, whom I knew to be a devoted church worker and a stout character. I went right on up to see her, and found her considerably weakened physically, but alert and far from depressed. I learned that, with her customary decisiveness and directness, she had willed her body to the medical school and wanted me to help her with the customary arrangements, filling out the proper forms, etc. When we were through with these, she said, "Ah! That's a relief! That was the only thing left to do. My will is in order, and my pastor knows the kind of memorial service I want. So now I don't have to worry."

In the days that followed, although she gradually became weaker, she was quietly content. I was able to get the doctor to see that, far from being morbid, the woman was at peace; and he found, to his surprise, that he could talk to her about dying without his previous feelings of alarm. The patient did as much for him as he was able to do for her.

Of course, not every patient can face death this way. Nor can those who love and serve him always be sure of their own ability to discuss such arrangements objectively. In many cases, it simply is not necessary because of the depth of tacit understanding that is shared by all, and the unwavering security that is provided by loving care. When a patient facing death is sustained by the support of people whom he trusts, he may be content to leave all arrangements in their hands.

But there are many other patients who need the opportunity to discuss arrangements. It is not so much the thought of death that fills them with dismay (for death often comes to them as a welcome release), as it is the fear of leaving things undone, of breaking off with loose ends hanging, of losing control over self and possessions. For such people it is of the utmost importance to participate in the disposition of their own affairs. When they become aware that death is approaching, it can be extremely troubling not to have everything in order.

When, out of our own fear of appearing morbid, we shut out any discussion of arrangements, we do the patient a great disservice. If, on the other hand, we can assist in helping to make the arrangements requested, we do the patient great honor, and, in effect, liberate him to live out the remainder of his days in quietness and self-respect.

ANTICIPATORY GRIEF

THE EDITORS

No amount of foreknowledge of grieving will do more than mitigate the event of death when it comes. But the presence of grief in anticipation of the loss alters its subtle progression; the inevitable change has foreshadowed one's feelings; one is powerless, and a measure of resignation has crept in. A sorrowful reality is about to ensue; and actual death comes as an affirmation of his pre-knowledge. Sharp grief has already been experienced; but the sharpest edge of grief comes at this time. However, because of his anticipatory grief, the bereaved more readily finds his way back to peace, according to the dictates of his own situation and the ensuing circumstances. Those about him should somehow be brought to the same realization, so that they will understand all the bereaved's reactions to the ultimate event and will become better able to assist, rather than hinder him in working through his grief.

Thus, without recognition of the influence of anticipatory grief, no consideration of the complexities constituting the transcendent emotional and physical state of bereavement would be complete. Hence, once the bereaved and those about him become aware that grief in anticipation of the death of a loved one does, in fact, occur, a giant stride toward recovery will have been made.

D. COPING WITH GRIEF

HOW TO UNDERSTAND GRIEF

Robert A. Edgar

How do we understand and rise above grief when death takes a loved one? It is important for us to understand that the psychological effect of grief on our emotions is in many ways similar to the physical effects of surgery on our bodies. Take as an example the removal of a major organ of the body. There normally follow three days of critical condition as the body makes a tremendous adjustment. There are seven days of hospital and nursing care, and then there are likely to be two weeks of solid rest at home. Depending upon the seriousness of the surgery, there are apt to be three months' convalescing and rebuilding of the body as it adjusts to the loss of the organ. There is no way for the physician or the nurse or the family or the patient to speed up this process. It just takes this long for God's healing power to take effect. What a wonderful healing power God has put in us! We rejoice in it, but we cannot change its tempo.

The grief process has a similar sequence. If we understand it and accept it, each of us will be prepared to face his own grief. Then, in a very real sense, we will be able to reach out and touch with faith and understanding someone who is going through this sequence, however protracted it may be.

It seems to me there are five phases that most people pass through as they go through what is commonly known as the "work of grief."

First of all, there is the phase that is called *the numbness of the whole being*. This comes at the beginning, especially when death is sudden. The whole mind and spirit become insensitive to feeling, anesthetized, as the person really moves out of awareness of what is going on. This is a wonderful plan of God's to permit the whole psychophysical mechanism to have time to absorb the bad news. One is in a semi-stupor, with little realization of what's happening.

In this first stage, how does one help a person who is in this state of shock? It does no good to discuss religion or to tell him what you believe. The important thing is to *be there*. And if you want to say, "I've come to be with you because my heart aches with you," that's fine. Try to understand how the person is feeling. You can't really—

but try. And he will know that you are trying, and in this semi-conscious state he will rejoice that someone cares. You may do the practical, natural things, such as bringing in the food and surrounding the family with physical comforts and necessities.

During this stage of numbness, one just waits, waits until the next stage, which is called the phase of fantasy-reality. This comes as the numbness of the shock begins to wear off and the mind begins to have some feelings. As the mind reaches this condition, it tries to build a dike against the reality. We find ourselves saying, "It isn't true. It can't be. I won't believe it." And yet on the other hand we say, "Well, all these people are here, and he's not here. I won't believe it and yet I must."

Then there is the hard struggle of the dreams about the one we loved. For try as hard as we can, we live at night in our sleep as if our loved one is alive. No one who has not experienced the bereavement dream can possibly understand the struggle of grief in this phase of fantasy and reality.

It is tremendously important to move through this second stage and reality, for as long as one remains in the dream world, life is unreal and there is no progress through grief. At first agreeing with those who said it was better to remember the loved one as he was in life, I had not always thought it wise for the bereaved to view a body. I am convinced now, after many years of relating to people in this stage of grief, that it is important to break the fantasy/reality conflict and to view the body, hard as it may be. Adjustment is delayed if one continues too long in the fantasy world.

How does one help another go through this second stage of grief? Again, by just being there to comfort and to love. What you say does not really matter, as long as you do not preach or advise or minimize the reality. We help the person endure the pain but we cannot take it from him by encouraging him in the fantasy, such as saying "he isn't really dead, he's just not here." There is a time for this kind of understanding, but it is much later. We need to help break through the fantasy/reality struggle.

The person goes into the third phase, exemplified by various psychological reactions that are natural but sometimes repulsive to those who listen. There are *feelings* of *desertion* and *rejection*. It is natural for human beings to feel sorry for themselves. We are basically selfish. And at a time like this, without realizing it, in this process of healing through grief we are apt to find ourselves saying, "In the middle of everything he just lay down and died. We have so much to do together and look, he's gone off and left me."

When one feels this way, one needs to express it. And one certainly should not have someone remonstrate: "You shouldn't be talking this way." For a person needs to be honest with his feelings if he passes through a reaction of rejection and desertion.

Or again, there is the feeling of *anger*. "Why should this happen to me? God, You did this to me and it isn't fair." No one should say, "Don't you condemn God": God understands and accepts our anger.

Or there are the feelings of *guilt* that are so hard to rise above. "There must have been something I could have done. I should have made him rest more. I should have insisted that he take that vacation. I used to nag him about all the little things. Oh, how I wish I could tell him how much I love him." These are real feelings and they are natural. We must get them out. Those who surround us must accept them as natural, not giving advice, not condemning, not contradicting, not correcting, not giving one's own philosophy or religious views. The bereaved does not need this. He needs someone to love him and to accept him as he struggles through the natural process of the normal psychological reaction of a human being being jerked through *the most difficult, trying and tragic experience of life.*

Now we move into the fourth phase of grief, which I call *the flood of grief*. The dike breaks and the pressure of reality wins out. Emotion overflows with weeping and tears. This should be expected and encouraged. The admonition to "be brave," or the feeling that we ought to be brave can be dangerous. This flood of grief may come earlier for some, but it must come. It may last longer for some than for others, depending on the suddenness of the death and the emotional condition of the bereaved. But it must come. This is the way God has of helping a person find acceptance, as he is able to give vent to his built-up feeling of loss.

If this phase of grief is missed, we have been told by many people that it will come out later on, probably in abnormal reactions with permanent maladjustments to life. People in our society try to be brave all their lives. They have never been honest with their true feelings. They build a hard crust around their feelings and emotions. This crust often shatters in unfortunate circumstances.

Now we come to the last phase, and of course the most important. It is essential to reach this phase if we are to have a healthy life.

If we have come through the first four stages (and most of us do), then we need as far as is possible to carry on as before trusting in God's care. How does one do this?

Some people feel that they should change their whole way of life. They should sell the home, go to another climate, try to escape the past. How tragic this is. Those who die ahead of us want us to carry on as before. Think of our need for friends who know us. How important it is to stay near them!

How important it is to rejoice in memories. It is difficult at first. Go to the familiar holiday spot as usual. There will be a terrific lonesomeness for a while, but soon this will give way to the feeling that you are not alone. It is right to sense his presence because you have gone through the fantasy/reality stage and you know what is real. Sometimes this feeling of his presence is more real than some of the other experiences which are so important to us.

Pull out the familiar books you have enjoyed together. Read them again. Put on the familiar hi-fi records. Carry on as before if it is possible.

One needs to re-examine the awareness of one's purpose in life for a healthy conclusion of grief. When Madam Curie's husband was killed in an automobile accident right on the verge of the great discovery, the medical use of radium, what did she do? She carried on where he had left off, and all humanity has benefited. Why? Because she worshipped God even more than she did her husband.

The trouble with us, and this is the hardest part, is we come to worship our loved ones. They become gods for us. And when a "god" dies, we are lost. "Thou shalt have no other gods before me!"

How essential it is for us to rediscover our true vocation as a Christian: Not our jobs, not our professions or our trades, but our lives of love in whatever profession or trade we may have.

When Abraham Lincoln was in the White House, one of his greatest joys during the troubled hours was his beloved son, Willy. When Willy succumbed to a fever, the President cried out in grief, "It is hard, it is hard to have him die." He reeled with the blow but recovered and returned to his vocation. Lincoln renewed his awareness of his calling.

How important it is for us, when we go through this valley of the shadow, to discover anew why we are here. Those who have been through the valley and have discovered again their purpose in Life are well along the way of completing the grief process.

WHY DID THIS HAPPEN TO ME?

DAVID J. SELIGSON

One of the most heartwarming and spiritually enriching experiences for a minister, priest, or rabbi is to feel that he and his congregation are united in faith and in bonds of the warmest personal relationship. Frequently, these bonds become the channels through which experience of the trials and tribulations of life is transmitted from one to another, as harassed individuals are faced with the desolation and grief of tribulation or bereavement.

I became gratefully aware of this when I received, a few weeks ago, a letter from a member of our congregation which reads in part: "Dear Rabbi—Some day I would like you to tell me why those I esteem so highly suffer so many trials and tribulations. Or is it that the suffering of people brings them closer to God and fills them with the human kindness which endears them to others?"

How often is this agonizing question wrung from people; and how often is it probed by doctors who fight the devastating inroads of incurable disease, by the bereaved who are made desolate by a sudden and untimely death, by the lonely and the stricken in spirit, and by those in whom the bitterness of despair becomes a corrosive cynicism and a denial of God and faith? *Why did this happen to me?*

It is to the everlasting credit of our ancient faith that it has faced these questions with mature realism. It has offered no anodynes, no watchwords or glib formulas with which to whitewash the cruelties of life. It has even enshrined human travail and the questionings and probings of God's justice in its book of faith. To all the generations of men it says: "Look! This is our book of faith, our lexicon of affirmations, our beliefs and our creeds. Here also is the unanswered question, the perennial searchings of the human spirit."

Thus Job, "the man who was wholehearted and upright that feared God and shunned evil," reeling from a succession of blows dealt him by a cruel fate, cries out in his agony:

"Let the day perish wherein I was born,
And the night wherein it was said:

'A man-child is brought forth'
Let that day be darkness . . .
Why died I not from the womb?
Why did I not perish at birth?"

And from that extraordinary skeptic, the author of the Book of Ecclesiastes, come these bitter, bitter words:

"All things I have I have seen in the days of my vanity:
There is a righteous man that perisheth in his righteousness, and
There is a wicked man that prolongeth his life in his evil-doing."

The Greek mind also created a legend—that of Prometheus. He was chained to a rock by the god Zeus, and an eagle plucked at his liver as punishment for stealing fire from heaven. The "Prometheus Bound" of Aeschylus is Hebraic in its moral tone. Like the Book of Job, it articulates the universal cry of man, his protest against his tragic lot.

I know of no theology that has adequately answered this cry from the human heart. Several years ago, a minister, a priest, and I were invited to share in a symposium which attempted to deal with these perennial questions. None of our efforts provided a definitive answer. Some forms of Christian evangelism maintain that the sorrows visited upon mortals are a punishment for sin, for which the only remedy is salvation through Christ. Buddhism offers a way of escape through absorption in the "All." But Judaism frankly admits that it has no answer for "the suffering of the righteous and the prosperity of the wicked." Indeed, there is an interesting discussion, recorded in the Talmud, as to whether life is worth living at all. The conclusion is reached that it were better for man not to have been born. But, since it is God's will that he be created, "Let him search his ways." Yet, the affirmation of life, the acceptance of its challenge, is a pervasive element in our tradition. Perhaps this dichotomy impelled the late Professor Schechter to comment that "the best theology is that which is not consistent, and this advantage, the theology of the synagogue possesses to its utmost extent."

What, then, emerges from our inquiry into the age-old question that has always tormented man? First of all, we must acknowledge that *we do not know* the meaning of life and *yet,* that we may someday *come* to know. Do not forget that only recently have we become familiar with such terms as Salk vaccine, atomic energy, penicillin, antibiotics, and other specifics that have shed light on the underlying cause of diseases against which we have had no adequate defense until today.

True, the area of the unknown is vast and incalculable and we are still groping in the dark; but, little by little, the light is beginning to penetrate the dark places.

"Be strong and of good courage," we say to all the bewildered, the saddened, the bereaved. Life is not designed for our comfort. Man travels a rough road. A measure of tragic heroism makes it possible for a man to go forward into life and to accept its responsibilities even though the burden is heavy. Thus, in our tradition, special merit was accorded to Abraham, our Father, of whom it is said, after the death of his beloved Sarah, "and Abraham arose from the face of his dead." Because he had the courage to rise from his dead and go forth into life, he is especially honored.

Our common human experience affirms the truth which was enunciated by a beloved and revered colleague, the late Milton Steinberg: "All life is a great fellowship of anguish in which each of us participates in some fashion or other." One of us suffers pain of the body; another terrors of the mind, the fear of insanity, or agonies of inferiority and insecurity. The heart of a third aches with loneliness, friendlessness. A fourth is tormented by remorse for old mistakes, errors, sins. Yet one more devours himself alive with jealousy and malice. Still another is haunted by a sense of pointlessness, being one of those multitudes who, as Thoreau put it, "live out lives of quiet desperation." And the moral inference is a simple, natural deduction from the tragic fact: the thesis that since all things suffer, all things merit our pity.

These are the things we do need—*a mature mind* which will not permit us to rage in impotence against the universe as though we had been chosen to be its special victim; *faith* in the ever-widening horizon of human knowledge and the capacity of the scientific world to unravel its mysteries; *courage* to recognize that life itself involves prob-

113

lems to be solved and tragedies to be endured; an *awareness* of the essential kinship of our common human travail and its challenge to our sympathy for and understanding of the sufferings of others; and, if we can muster it, *the faith* to say with the psalmist—"I shall not die but live and declare the works of the Lord. The Lord hath chastened me sore, but He hath not given me over unto death."

ACCEPTING THE FACT

MARVIN GOLDFINE

For one who feels a loss deeply, it is almost inevitable that the illusion of not really being separated should take possession of his mind as a protection against harsh reality. It is wise to be aware of this phenomenon and to reckon with it. Illusion tends to feed on itself, and can grow quickly to dangerous proportions.

Acceptance of the fact of death does not come easily, but no return to normal functioning is possible until it has been accomplished. Upon it depends one's ability to make the proper adjustments in his mode of life. What is virtually at stake is the achievement of a new balance in one's orientation to reality.

This is not to say that initial shock, deep grief or guilt are to be suppressed as abnormal or evil in themselves. They are in most cases unavoidable. What can be borne in mind is the desirability of minimizing and keeping them within bounds, in order to make way for the process of recovery to follow its course.

What could be helpful in the cultivation of acceptance is an awareness of the genuine worth of each individual, not only as a precious and unique being but also as one whose very nature and even glory reside in the fact that he or she is human and fine. Man might be defined as a being who knows he must die. It is each man's destiny to end his earthly sojourn, often leaving unfinished work and concerns behind, and terminating human relationships that had seemed so solid. If the survivor is to carry on in a more effective way, he or she may find indispensable support in a general orientation which balances a basic appreciation of each man's worth with an awesome sense of the frailty and transitoriness of life.

SEVEN CONCEPTS OF JACKSON'S WORKING FAITH

AUSTIN I. MEHRHOF

Perhaps the bereaved person derives the greatest comfort from within, from his faith, but it must be a working faith. In his book, *Understanding Grief*, Edgar N. Jackson outlines the seven concepts which constitute the minimum requirements for such a faith.

First, it is essential to have a purpose in life that will give one's own life and the lives of others significant meaning. Second, it is essential to have an understanding of man's unique spiritual nature, which gives him a place of responsibility in God's world. Third, one must understand and believe in the essential goodness of God. Fourth, one must understand that death is a relative concept and that there are values greater than physical existence. If one can understand this, he will be able to look upon death as the natural flow toward an end and not, in itself, as an ending. Fifth, if one is a Christian, he must have faith in Jesus who was the embodiment of the redeeming nature of God. Sixth, one's faith must be fortified by the concept of a historical continuity with those who have worshipped the same God and believed in the same values. Finally, seventh, a belief in the immortality of the soul is essential to faith. Implicit in this is the belief that while death is the final limit of one's physical existence, it also marks the entrance of the soul into eternal life.

A faith which is based on such concepts is, indeed, a faith which will be comforting and sustaining in times of grief and bereavement.

DEALING WITH GRIEF

Gerald C. Hammon

As a clergyman, I have shared in the grief experiences of many families, including my own. There is profound grief when death has been expected, and possibly even when it has been hoped for because of the suffering caused by terminal illness, just as there is grief when death, in senseless fashion, strikes down a young person. Death is not easy on anyone who is left behind.

I have found during my years in the ministry that certain contemporary conventions concerning the behavior of the bereaved tend to hinder in the process of working one's way through grief. To a degree we do need commonly accepted behavioral patterns to help us through the strain accompanying bereavement. Yet one such convention, for instance, that emotion should not be displayed, is most damaging. I feel that we must be willing to express and face our emotions when confronted by the death of a beloved one. Our society deems it quite proper to express publicly the happy emotions, joy, elation, or affection. But expressions of pain, anger, and sensitivity are not acceptable as public behavior. Yet, to work through our grief, to arrive at a new balance of life, to live with any degree of happiness, we must find release from the overpowering emotions of grief.

Since a sense of unreality and bewilderment follows the loss of a loved one, perhaps the most immediate task before us is simply to accept the reality of death. I recall one parishioner, who had lost her husband after over fifty years of marriage, saying that the whole situation seemed so unreal to her that at any moment she just knew he would come walking in the door.

In order to accept death, one must be able to talk about it. Many people try their best to keep the bereaved from even mentioning the death for fear of an emotional scene. Yet when death occurs, we do need to talk about it. We need to describe the events surrounding it in order to grasp its reality. At first these events cannot be recounted without displaying considerable emotion, but it is far more harmful to bottle up these emotions.

119

In fact, I usually worry about the person who is taking death "wonderfully." The person who sails through the whole experience with apparent serenity can have a terrific backlash of emotion at some future date, or can eventually show signs of having never truly accepted the death.

Many of us who officiate at funerals have had the experience of observing someone who is only distantly related to the deceased break down and display signs of grief as severe as those of more intimate members of the family. On closer examination, we usually find that this individual had suffered a loss at some time in the past, but his grief had never been worked out or fully expressed. The current occasion had triggered expression of the repressed grief; the process of working through the earlier grief had finally been begun. I might add that the task is made harder because the person does not understand why he is reacting in this manner. Difficult as it may seem, death must be faced at the time it occurs if we are not to fall into an emotional booby trap at a later time.

The task of working our way through grief is not meant to enable us to forget but to make it possible for us to recall memories of the deceased without being overwhelmed by pain or emotion. By expressing and accepting our feelings of grief, we will ultimately be able to go on living without being emotionally tied to the event of death. We will not then fall heir to needless feelings of guilt over what we might or might not have done for or to the deceased.

Working our way through grief leads to an understanding of the self. It permits us to create new relationships without feeling unfaithful to the old. God has made mankind with the need for meaningful relationships. He has given us the capacity for joy as well as for sorrow. He has redeemed grief from being an expression of hopeless loss by His promise of an Eternal Life. To work through grief adequately, the bereaved must foster his faith that the lost one is not really lost but is present within God's greater Kingdom. We can look forward to a renewal of fellowship and love in God's own way and in His own time.

WHAT COMES AFTER THE FUNERAL

Usually there is very little about the deceased person that the minister can tell people assembled for the funeral service.

The purpose of the funeral service is to bring a word of honest comfort and consolation to the family of the deceased and to his friends, to assure them that solace can come from God, and to offer a fervent and sincere prayer that the Almighty may strengthen their hearts and their courage for the difficult days ahead.

Such a funeral service offers beautiful, quiet, respectful homage to the power of a loved one's personality. It becomes a victory of the spirit over the attack of death. It becomes a tribute of yearning affection on the part of friends who have come to pay their respects, to stand by the family in sorrow, to be able to express by their presence at the funeral what is on their silent lips: "We, too, have suffered a loss; we, too, share in your sense of grief."

People often make the mistake of thinking that as soon as the funeral is over, they have to start disposing of things, making plans, selling this, getting rid of that, running away, taking a trip. They expend all kinds of nervous energy in trying to escape from the real problem of how they are going to live with the burden of their honest grief.

The study of psychology has taught us that grief is a complex emotion that must be allowed to come out. Unless it is brought to the surface and expressed, it can work severe damage on the individual, gnaw at his personality, and undermine the essential stability of his mental health. Repressing one's grief, submerging it, keeping it bottled up, does not put the painful and the unpleasant out of mind. Sometimes we see people in grief who are unable to settle down and who become moody, even neurotic, because they have been unable to come to grips realistically with their grief. Feelings of guilt, doubt, pain, dejection, hypocrisy, self-contempt, inner stress, all can do intense damage to our inner life. How false and phony our society is to think that a certain amount of grief, or a proper amount of crying,

121

must be exhibited to the public in order to demonstrate affection! Or the reverse, to think that sorrow must be controlled in order to demonstrate poise and courage and personal strength. A person has to work through his own grief, as Dr. Erich Lindemann has so wisely shown in his own scientific work on the subject. Only by evaluation of the experience of grief, by expression, by catharsis, by remembrance, by release, can a person be helped to help himself, so that a new self emerges out of the grief.

No, there is no embarrassment or shame in honest grief. It comes to all of us. A person in sorrow must not worry about what other people may think of him. The real person does not falsify his emotions to conform to someone else's idea of social convention. Grief is natural. It is human. It is universal.

After the funeral service is over, the person's first rush of overpowering grief is past. He probably thought he could never endure it, and yet a sense of relief comes to him as he knows that his beloved one is resting in peace. He becomes reconciled to knowing that nothing can bring his loved one back, for all he can do now is remember.

GRIEF AND HUMANITY

GENE E. BARTLETT

Someone has suggested that one of the best means of insight into another's real thinking is to see what he underlines in a book. It seems that we read according to our need. Our sight is selective. If so, anyone who has known sorrow would be arrested by a line in one of the *Sonnets to the Portuguese.* Elizabeth Barrett Browning, writing of her love for Robert, reaches into an unexpected area of experience to confess, "I love thee with all the passion put to use in my old griefs."

Even a glance at these words can touch all our questionings with hope. *Can* we find new outlets for all that "passion put to use in our old griefs?" The deepest personal crisis any one of us faces in his lifetime is the death of a loved one. The change with which we are faced is so final and so radical that the whole pattern of life is broken. If the deceased is that one with whom we have the closest interdependence, the result is nothing less than crisis. For the grieving, life can go either way. It can contract or expand, it can go back or go on, it can find new depths or new dimensions of faith.

Stated most simply, the issue seems basic: Will the grief absorb the person or will the person absorb the grief? If the former, then the life of the bereaved virtually comes to a standstill. There is loss of energy, a progressively demanding grief, a mounting self-absorption whose issue is a misery as intense as any known to man. But if, in due time, it is the person who absorbs the grief, then whole dimensions are added to his remaining years, dimensions which come only through the conquest of suffering. None of us would make such a statement lightly, for the pain of grief is too intense. But there is witness enough and more that such grief can make us more fully human.

When grief comes, the first longing—the first, intense longing—is that it be removed. It is the desperate hope that the underlying occasion of grief might be removed. One feels completely "caught." Actually, grief is not the problem, for when the occasion of death

123

comes, grief is the only appropriate and healing reaction. In itself, grief provides a new form of closeness to the loved one. To be without grief would be the ultimate loss, a kind of stark alienation.

But since grief cannot be removed, it still must be redeemed. Faith holds out to us the hope that it can be transmuted, put to other uses. More than that, faith bears witness that such transmuted grief endows life with new qualities. Faith presupposes a basic confidence in life's ultimate meaning; when we are thus supported, grief can be nothing less than a transcendent force. In the fullness of time it makes life different, bringing its own kind of clarification, assurance, and energy.

Then where do we put to use the passion of grief? To be sure, only the long view allows us to see how this comes about. One caught in the first paroxysm of sorrow may well ask with defiance how such passion could ever be transformed. But we are not without witness to the truth that grief really can make us more fully human.

For one thing, grief can become compassion. Biography and literature provide us with many witnesses to this truth. One of these concerns Sir William Osler in the days when he was working in the military hospitals of Britain during World War 1. Friends could remember that day when he was called out of the wards during his daily rounds to be given the word that his own son had been killed on the fields of France. They remembered that, stunned by this news, he still came back to pick up his rounds. For days the cheerful note was gone from his voice and they did not hear the tune which he often had whistled as he went from ward to ward. Though these never returned, something new came to take their place. Everyone noticed that a new compassion had come into his care of the soldiers who each day streamed in from the fields of France. Before, he had had the professional concern of the physician so important to the practice of medicine; now there was added that discernible note of a personal compassion, like that of a father for his son.

Others may remember a woman of very humble background. There is a statute to her memory in the city of New Orleans. It is the figure of a woman seated in a rocking chair, holding a child in her arms. The only carved word is the single name: Margaret. To those who lived in New Orleans at the time, the name was all that was necessary. For Margaret was a familiar figure throughout the city, known for one great passion, her love of children. As a young immigrant girl she had come to New Orleans to find a new home. In a few years she had married, then lost both her husband and her child. When bereavement came, she first took work in orphanages where she could help care for other children. Then, because of her skills in baking, she began to sell her goods, peddling them from a cart. She prospered in this, and her single place of business became a chain of bakeries. Yet Margaret never changed her basic style of life. Always, the proceeds from her business were used to maintain orphanages where children could find refuge. Today, the methods of Margaret would be considered far out of date, but the basic spirit of this woman is timeless and contemporary. Into her work went "all the passion put to use in her old griefs."

Is this not the way grief is redeemed, actually out of pain, making us more fully human? The bereaved discovers that his grief is part of the common human experience. He knows the democracy of suffering. This is the way human beings draw close to one another. Out of many, we become one through a common memory.

Grief also can become serenity. Perhaps we can eventually become serene because we feel that in facing the separation of death we have undergone life's ultimate test, and in the testing found our strength sufficient. The compensation is a new assurance, a sense of adequacy for future testings. Serenity in part is the assurance of sufficiency.

A. J. Gossip of Scotland preached a memorable sermon bearing witness to this truth. His marriage had been marked by a sustaining companionship clear to all in his congregation. Suddenly that companionship was broken by death. When Dr. Gossip returned to his pulpit for the first time after the loss of his wife, he chose the subject, "When Life Tumbles In, What Then?" Those who heard would never forget the closing lines as he spoke of the stream of sorrow through which he was passing: "I, too, like Hopeful, can call back to you who one day in your turn will have to cross it, 'Be of good cheer, my brothers, for I feel the bottom, and it is sound.'"

Perhaps this is what is meant by the strange Biblical phrase, "the peace that passes all understanding." There is a peace which is quite understandable; in fact, it is precisely what you would expect. It is the peace that comes when all is well, the relationships of life are intact, and the securities of life are undisturbed. But the peace that passes understanding is that which comes when the very opposite is true, when the relationships are broken and the securities have been taken away. That peace, once known, is never forgotten, and never fully taken away. Discovered in the midst of grief, it remains when the grief has passed its first anguished days.

Once more, grief can become motivation. We never will be able to measure that amount of the world's work for human welfare which has been made possible by the energies first released in sorrow. Perhaps it is motivation like that of the great Quaker philosopher Rufus Jones, who is reputed to have kept near him for forty years the portrait of a son who died as a small boy. Closest friends say that the philosopher never lost the sense that he must be a father whose life would be respected by a growing son.

In whatever form it may appear, the outlet for our sorrow often may lie in ministry to the wider needs of the world or in the unending battle against injustice. A world marked by such needs offers many saving outlets to those who must ask: Where do I use the passion put to use in my old griefs?

Just as morning actually begins a moment after midnight, when the whole world passes a meridian and begins to move not into deeper darkness but toward the light, so even in our sorrow, the newness of life begins long before we are aware of it. If we continue to trust and prepare for the fuller disclosure, we shall know that there is a word for us which is strange and paradoxical but true: Grief indeed can make us more fully human. And that is the highest gift we can receive.

AVOIDING THE PARALYSIS OF GUILT

Joseph C. Landrud

When we experience the death of someone close, one of our most common reactions is the feeling of guilt. This is especially true if the death is tragic in its suddenness, as in a traffic accident or suicide, or if the death is that of a child or an aged relative, someone who has required our care through crucial periods of life. Guilt is certainly not limited to these situations, however, and is present to some degree in all instances of bereavement.

At times of such sorrow we often tend to bombard ourselves with endless queries of "Oh, why didn't I do this" and "If I had only thought of that, it would never have happened." Such self-chastisement may be completely unrealistic, arising not out of the immediate cause of the death but, rather, derived from a whole series of previous events in relation to the one who had died which may only now take vivid expression. Or, the origin of such feelings may have nothing whatsoever to do with the one who has died, but may be a specific inclination in the personality structure of the mourner.

On the other hand, guilt feelings may be entirely realistic, growing out of one's personal awareness of responsibilities accepted and yet *not* discharged within the full range of one's capabilities. The sting of such awareness may be especially devastating.

However, whether such feelings of guilt are based upon reality or not, they are bound to exist in every person at the time of death in some proportion because of the very nature of man himself. For man is a "feeling" and self-aware creature and, as Paul Tillich has stated, "A profound ambiguity between good and evil permeates everything he does, because it permeates his personal being as such,—the awareness of this ambiguity is the feeling of guilt."[1]

Precisely because such a sense of guilt is part of the human condition, we should not be surprised when we experience it. Indeed,

---

1. Paul Tillich, *The Courage To Be*. Clinton, Mass., The Colonial Press, Inc., 1959, p. 52.

not to experience it should be cause for alarm, for its absence could only mean that we have felt no sense of mutuality with the deceased —no concern, no respect, no obligation, no responsibility. Can anyone be said to have an authentic relationship with another to any meaningful degree if all such significant dimensions are missing? The answer is obvious. Consequently, we should expect guilt feelings to accompany our loss of anyone to whom we have become committed by bonds of sharing. Whenever we give ourselves to another in love, which, in its deepest form, is the exposure of our own frightened vulnerability to the unconditioned response of another, and witness that love being returned in even greater measure than we dared anticipate, we are staggered with joy beyond description. Yet, when this same individual is taken from us in death, we are often consumed with images of what might have been; we rack our memories and sensitivities for instances wherein we erred, believing that in some unfathomable manner our own self-recriminations might restore him to us, or at least assuage our personal anguish.

If some degree of guilt is to be expected at times of bereavement, there are several salient points we should keep in mind in order to deal with it in the most constructive manner:

Feelings of guilt, whether based upon reality or not, are not necessarily a bad thing. They *can* be a positive force when used as signposts for learning, so that any mistakes made are not repeated. That is, the feelings of guilt must be faced and dealt with through examination of and verification with the real facts. The essential outlook, then, must be to face the past situation, deal with it in the present, and utilize the lessons learned in building the future.

The chief drawback in arriving at this outlook, however, is the difficulty experienced by many in not being able to *let go* of past guilt feelings. It is almost as if some people collected "guilt stamps," in the same manner as retail consumers collect Blue Chip and S & W Green Stamps.[2] That is, they are collected, stored in our subconscious just as we put the stamps in books, and then ultimately cashed

---

2. Eric Berne, M.D., discusses such "Trading Stamps" in his *Principles of Group Treatment*. New York, Oxford University Press, 1966, pp. 286-288.

in at the redemption store for a "prize," although all too often the "prize" is a destructive one: a depression, psychosis, or suicide. It is during this period of "collection" of guilt feelings, or "guilt stamps," that one begins to experience an increased lethargy or mounting loneliness, which can culminate in a state of social and/or emotional paralysis, for which the "payoff" (or punishment) is often some form of mental incapacity.

Although such guilt feelings themselves rightly fall within the framework of psychology, the way to avoid their paralyzing effect can most adequately be understood in terms of theology. That is, God alone can forgive us the guilts which paralyze; He alone can cleanse us of the acid of self-punishment which seems to eat away at our personalities; He alone can restore us to our internal equilibrium and to meaningful relationships with our fellow humans; He alone can accept us *as we are*, and this acceptance can give us the impetus to accept ourselves, to free us from our own enslavement. Then, our greatest problem becomes that of accepting the fact that we have been accepted, even though we may still feel unacceptable.

Guilt, in its essence, means the failure to accept ourselves. We are too quick to pinpoint our flaws, shortcomings, and mistakes, and we have the tendency to accentuate the negative characteristics of our thoughts and behavior. For our mental and emotional equilibrium and our continued functioning as responsible persons, we must counter this nonacceptance of ourselves, or guilt, with genuine self-acceptance. Such self-acceptance comes *not* from a denial of the guilt-producing situation, or the unhealthy suppression of it into our unconscious. Real self-acceptance can come only from *forgiveness*. Yet this forgiveness requires more than mere acknowledgment: It must be experienced and personally realized.[3]

But how can anyone so torn apart by guilt, in the depths of despair, at the furthest point from self-acceptance, repelled by anything concerning him personally, allow himself to even *think* about forgiveness?

---

3. James G. Emerson, Jr., deals with the problem of "realized forgiveness" as it pertains to second marriages in his *Divorce, The Church and Remarriage*. Philadelphia, The Westminster Press, 1961.

The solution to this dilemma is that the all-necessary forgiveness comes *not* from ourselves (in that our very guilt renders us to be anything but self-forgiving), but from God. He is the only One who can truly forgive. His forgiveness comes, not because of anything we have done to earn or merit it, but with no conditions attached. He does not deny or whitewash our guilt—He simply accepts it as we confess it to Him. And in the process of this amazing dynamic, he *accepts us*, as we are, and lifts us up out of our despondence. Only as we accept His acceptance, even while being fully aware of our own unacceptability, do we begin to enter into anything like a state of authentic self-acceptance. Only then are we freed from the paralysis of guilt.

COPING WITH BEREAVEMENT

Glenn R. Mosley

No one will accept, all at one time, the fact of a loved one's death. Rather, acceptance is usually accomplished in stepwise fashion.

Step 1. The loss of a loved one often produces a phenomenon which students of the mind's processes have called the *numbing effect.* In essence, this is the emotional inability, for a time, to accept in a realistic way the fact of death. Only gradually does the full reality of the loss of the loved one reach the bereaved. This is one of an All-Providing Wisdom's ways of helping the bereaved not to have to accept the full emotional impact of the loss of a loved one all at once. For most people, this would be an overwhelming experience.

Step 2. For some others, this overwhelming experience is avoided by the *bereavement dream.* The bereaved individual may have such vivid dreams of the deceased, that it is difficult to believe he has not actually returned. Gradually, however, these dreams change and the elements of hard reality become a part of the dream process. As it is with the waking feelings of disbelief, so the bereavement dream seems to help the deeply grieved to accept the full impact of loss in a way that is less devastating than the sudden and complete recognition of the fact of death would be.

Step 3. There is a recognizable pattern to the grief emotions which are a part of mourning, and it is a complete one. The first and most poignant feeling is, of course, a *sense of loss.* If the departed one was a member of our immediate family, we see him on every side, doing the things he did in everyday life, with a deep realization that he is no longer present to share these experiences of life. We grieve that the loved one can no longer share the joys of life. At the same time, we feel loneliness, emptiness, and a painful sadness at having to face life without the person we have known so long and loved so deeply. Another set of feelings revolves around our anxiety at being faced with sudden change. We are not sure what lies ahead. Concern about our own death lurks relentlessly in the back of our minds, and we fear the frightening unknown.

Step 4. That fear often gives birth to anger. *Fear and anger,* especially in bereavement, are twins. That is, we may be at a loss about what to do next in very practical matters. We may feel help-lessly confused and angry that Fate chose such tribulations for us to experience. Our anger may keep us from facing the problems and fears that actually gave rise to the anger. We may say that these reactions are childish; however, there is nothing wrong with having childish reactions when one is first faced with an experience that is overwhelming. By understanding that these childish reactions are likely to occur, we are well on the way toward a more positive and mature way of handling our problems and our grief.

Step 5. We must try to solve the *practical problems*: Where shall we live, how shall we pay our bills, how shall we find a degree of security in a world that has suddenly changed so drastically? The future may seem threatening and uncertain. Sometimes we make decisions by ourselves—decisions that were always shared before. This in itself causes more insecurity and uncertainty.

———

At the beginning of the second semester of my freshman year in college, I moved from the dormitory to a private home, where I shared a large room with two other boys—another freshman, Bob, and a senior, Bruce. The couple who owned the home were retired. Mr. T. had been with the railroad and Mrs. T. had been a school teacher.

Since the T.'s had not been able to have children, taking in boys from the university was more than just a means to obtain a little added income. In a way, it allowed them to be the parents they had always wanted to be. As often happens with couples without children, the T.'s were very close to each other, perhaps even exces-sively dependent on each other.

Two weeks after I moved into the home, Mr. T. was killed by a train. Within a few hours, distant relatives came to stay with Mrs. T. There was little that we three boys could do that was not being done, but we helped whenever possible. On Tuesday evening, the day before the funeral, Bob, Bruce, and I went to the chapel to pay our respects. Since I was the pre-theology major among us, I was selected to express our condolences to the beloved lady.

I approached her and tried four or five times to say something that would be meaningful. But everything that occurred to me seemed impossibly trite. Finally, I just put my arm around her; she literally "cried on my shoulder." I stood beside her several minutes; then kissed her cheek and retreated.

Later, Bruce asked, "If you are going to be a minister, what will you say to the bereaved?"

My honest answer was, "I don't know, Bruce, I just do not know." I was sixteen years old at the time.

Years of training and years of experience with the bereaved, and deep, personally felt grief have taught me some answers to help meet bereavement. I find it is best to approach the bereaved, put your arms around him, let him literally "cry on your shoulder" if he wants or needs to, give him either verbal or tacit assurance of your caring and concern, and, in time, retreat.

Failure of Concepts of Life

There are very few to whom psychological, philosophical, or theological concepts mean very much in the early stages of grief. No matter how rational they seem or how scientifically sound the theories may be at any other time of the bereaved's life, at that sad time, the concepts are empty. The heart cries out and is not comforted with easy answers.

Contrasts and Changes in Life

From infancy on, we are faced with contrasts. The infant learns to distinguish light from darkness. He learns to differentiate between hot and cold, dry and wet, pain and comfort, joy and sorrow; later he is taught right from wrong; good from bad. At some point in life, that child or adult faces the fact of death, usually vicariously, at first, and then personally, even though his own death is likely to be many years away.

To understand better the meaning of the experience which we call death, we must understand better the experience we call life. Viewing any stage or level of life, we see that life is constantly changing. But with all the changes, life does not cease. The infant dies away that the young child may be born; the young child dies away that the adolescent may be born; the adolescent dies away that the young adult may be born; the young adult dies away that the older adult may be born into the perpetual maturation process. And, eventually, the body dies.

While it is both natural and important for the human heart to grieve when deprived of the daily association with a beloved one, it is important, too, to be reminded that the body is but the housing of the soul and the responsive heart and mind that we really love.

If several people were assembled in the living room of a large house which had many rooms and one of those people left the room, promising not to leave the house, the rest of the assembly might not know which of the many rooms he had entered, but would know only that he was still in that great house with them. This is true, too, with the passing of a loved one. There are many rooms in the great house of life. Our loved one enters a new dimension; one which we can neither share nor accurately evaluate from our own experience.

Just as it is a matter of perspective that causes a highway to appear to come to an end as we view it from a distance, so it is a matter of perspective which causes that which we call death to be an apparent end to life. As we move closer to the point in the highway which appeared to be the end, we find that the road may turn to the right or left, or it may continue straight ahead, but it does not end. The same is true with life; it continues in different degrees and at various levels, but it does not end. With all its changes, life never ceases; life only changes shape and form.

However, even with these theological or philosophical views concerning the continuation of life, we still must face the fact of death: our own and that of our loved ones. Although life does not cease, it becomes formless and disappears from the sight of life on this plane. It is this change which causes us to grieve.

BODY IMAGE AND GRIEF RESPONSE

Edgar N. Jackson

I.

The effort to understand more clearly what takes place in the processes of grief has led to interesting psychological research. Because grief involves the deepest feelings and the most profound emotions, it is not easily understood. It is so basic a part of life that it would be comparable to the emotions of mother love and self-preservation.

Dr. Robert Fulton has helpfully moved us one step of the way toward understanding what is involved in grief by his effort to illuminate the concept of identification. In its broadest usage, identification and love are synonymous. When you love people, you enter into their thoughts and feelings and value them as you value yourself. Their feelings become your feelings, and when they are injured or suffer, you are injured and suffer, too. When they feel joy and satisfaction, you also feel joy in their joy and satisfaction in their satisfaction.

The processes by which identification takes place are rooted in the individual's sense of selfhood, but they are fulfilled in the realization that the social self is never completed until it has significant relationships with another. In these relationships, a wide variety of experiences enrich and deepen the interpersonal processes of life. Friendship, interests shared mentally, physically, and spiritually, common activities and emotional fulfillment are the grounds from which identification develops. In order to understand the fullest meaning of identification, we have to move a step backward in the emotional processes, for our capacity for identification with the life of another is based on the nature and development of our own body image. A person who hates his own body would find it difficult to show respect and love for the body of another. Rather, his hatred would tend to produce the perverted emotions of sadism, which would injure the body of another and find enjoyment in that emotionally rooted assault. Similarly, the person who values his own body and treats it with respect would find it quite reasonable and natural to value and respect and love the body of another.

As grief is the other side of the coin of love—and we can truly grieve for another when we have truly loved and identified with that other person—we see how basic the concept of body image is to the understanding of the processes of grief. How does one develop a body image? How does a healthy body image complicate the life of an individual and make it difficult for him to cope with the powerful emotion of grief?

Psychiatrists have been working for years to understand the origins and nature of the body image. They have developed a variety of theories related to it, and some of these may be useful in our study. The psychiatrist tries to understand what is going on in the mental and emotional life of his patients. In order to develop this insight, he examines influences that shaped the mental and emotional life of the individual he treats. When he finds a correspondence in the developmental processes that affect a number of patients, he tends to develop a theory that explains what he observed. Let us now look at some of these theories for the light they throw on the concept of body image.

Years ago, Sigmund Freud, in his effort to unearth the roots of emotional disturbances, tried to understand how certain ideas and responses take root in life. He surmised that young children were more sensitive and impressionable than most adults assumed. The general attitude of his day was that children were not able to learn anything until they were old enough to talk and reason. But in his clinical experience it seemed to be the very opposite, for the emotional patterns for life appeared to be quite well set while children were young, and many of the feeling responses seemed to be acquired before a child could talk.

In his efforts to elaborate his theory of the early acquisition of mental and emotional characteristics, Dr. Freud gave prominence to the idea that should have been obvious but was largely overlooked, that children at an early age are completely dependent upon others, have strong feelings, and are not only sensitive to the feelings of those around them, but also are singularly vulnerable to the feelings of others because they have not yet developed any forms of protection against emotional assault.

For instance, a baby that was dearly loved and the center of tender and loving attention became emotionally secure and felt a sense of his own value, not in words but in feelings. When he was sung to, cooed over, and affectionately snuggled to his mother's breast, he developed a feeling about himself that was accepting and good. But if the opposite were true, and the child were treated with disgust, neglected and handled roughly and without love, the child would show anxiety, insecurity and other symptoms of hazardous feelings about himself. These feelings planted in the early stages of life would tend to condition the emotional responses for the rest of life, and the child as a result would be anxiety-free or anxiety-ridden, self-confident or filled with feelings of inferiority.

These deep and early feelings about himself are the stuff of which the body image is built. Freud said that "what is laid down inside is an image of what is perceived outside." Memory is not dependent upon recall, but may be built into the emotional responses at such a basic level of life that the result is almost an automatic response to new experience. Freud spoke of this as the "body ego" but, for easier comprehension, it is now generally referred to as body image.

This concept is an internalized amalgamation of the accumulated unconscious, preconscious and subconscious experience of the organism in its response to the life process. The anxious and insecure tend to draw from this reservoir of experience a reaction that shows up in defensive behavior, just as those who draw from the same reservoir the responses of self-acceptance and creative confidence, indicate their past experience of security and acceptance by others.

Let us illustrate the way this psychological principle manifests itself in human behavior. A well-known actress was considered to be exceedingly beautiful, so much so that she was portrayed in moving pictures, barracks, and magazine covers as the epitome of feminine atractiveness. But the way others saw her did not correspond with her own idea of herself. Her background in early life had been marred by family discord, family breakdown, and ensuing experiences which she interpreted as rejection. The whole world acclaimed and accepted her as a sex symbol, but deep within herself she still considered herself to be an unwanted and undesirable person. Her self-image and her body image were quite different from those that others attributed to her. So powerfully did these deep inner forces influence her life that she was unable really to relate the acclaim to herself but rather was overwhelmed with the inner image of herself that dominated her inner life. The victory of the inner image was so complete that ultimately she could not tolerate the self that she had to live with, and she committed suicide. The unhealthy body image and self-image that had been built up in preverbal life experience appeared to be so dominant that it overwhelmed the later experience which had emphasized a completely different form of group response to her as a person.

Quite in contrast has been the experience of another well-known actress. She is not particularly beautiful, in fact, she is rather plain looking. But she comes from a background of culture and security, emotionally and socially. She has never known a time when she was not valued as a person. In early life she was wanted and loved. The experience of her first years of life was marked by warmth, acceptance, security and an all-pervading sense of her personal worth. Now that she has been a successful actress for decades, she shows the inner durableness of the person who can handle stress because her self-image and body image are accepting and tend to correspond with the feelings that people have of her. The strength of her inner being is at work for her, rather than the weakness of her inner being working against her.

Though these contrasting illustrations may oversimplify the matter of body image, they do point out one thing that is important: that the body image becomes an important resource with wise and health-ful living. When the body image is marred early in life, emotional hazards are created that can plague life at every point. But when the body image is sound, rooted in self and group acceptance, and in clear correspondence with reality, it becomes a resource for meeting whatever life brings to the individual, whether it be moments of joyful acceptance or times of emotional crises.

II.

As the depth and significance of feelings in life are related to the individual's feelings about himself, we can see how healthy feelings about the self tend to produce more healthful emotional relationships with others. The roots of these feelings in early life were enunciated by Freud but were elaborated upon by some of his followers with greater detail. These theories show how the attitudes of adults toward death become important factors in the unconscious response of the child to death. Once planted, the emotional problem persisted through the years.

John S. came to my attention when he was about to graduate from the theological seminary. He was concerned that his fear of death and funerals would affect his ministry. He had never been to a funeral; he felt a sickening chill go up and down his spine when a funeral coach drove by, and would walk blocks out of his way to avoid passing a funeral home. John's father had been killed in an industrial accident when he was three-years-old. He had been told nothing about the event, but could not be protected from the emotional turmoil that surrounded it. As he was an only child, his mother was overprotective and actually clung to him emotionally to fill the void left by the father's death. John had been close to his father. The idea of death to him at that early age was one of painful deprivation. Because he was so young, he saw no clear distinction between physical and emotional pain. The word death, or anything that reminded him of it, produced an immediate and diffused reaction of discomfort. His defense, copied after that of his mother, was to try to avoid the verbal or visual stimuli that caused his unpleasant response. His body image was confused with that of his father. Because his mother would never answer his questions or discuss the matter, it became even more anxiety-creating. His body image was so involved in his grief for his father that he had never been able to make a separation. The process counseling that ensued sought to bring the confused emotional state to the surface so that his feelings could be discussed and sorted out. On this basis a new understanding developed, and he was able to separate his own basic feelings from the event that involved his father. In essence, he was able to free himself from the physical pain of his father's death. When that was done, he moved beyond the threat involved, and was able to separate the death of any individual from the generalized anxiety that surrounded death as a persistent threat to his body image and self-image.

139

Then he was able to see other people and their needs in such a way that he could perform his pastoral duties wisely and well.

This case illustrates the condition that exists when a person is so completely identified with another at the level of body image that he is overwhelmed with the pains of grief and the fears of death. In effect, the death happens to him personally, and he has little or no protection against the painful feelings that are continually related to the fact of death. Only when the person is able to move beyond his own body image to the place where he can see with certainty that the death has happened to another and not to himself, is he able to be freed from anxiety, physical pain and emotional hazard.

Another way of illuminating the powerful emotional force related to body image or body identification is found in that complicated but basic drive we call mother love. We recognize that there is no human relationship wherein the body identification of one person is so close to another as in the process of gestation. It is doubly significant, for it tends to fulfill the powerful drives of sex and at the same time to produce new and significant body feelings between baby and mother. The pregnant mother often finds a meaning for her existence that she cannot find anywhere else. In fact, she may be able to value her body only when it is engaged in this procreative process. As one physician put it, "For many women it is only when they are pregnant or breast-feeding that they really value their own bodies and know how to love themselves—for it is only by identifying with the child that they feel worthy of love."

This makes it possible to understand the powerful emotions of loss and despair that often appear at the death of a young child. More significantly than we are apt to realize, this loss diminishes the meaning of life itself, especially for the mother. The strong body identification is fractured at the point where it brings together several powerful emotional drives. In consequence, the grief process is one of the most difficult to cope with, not only because it must contend with important unconscious and instinctual forces, but also because it tends to threaten the value structure of the persons most acutely aware of the loss.

Two psychological theoreticians have tried to develop their theories with a special interest in the mother-child identification and its relation to the self-image and that basic constituent of the self-image which we call body image.

Otto Rank was a student of Freud, but he felt that the base for Freud's theories was not broad enough. In his clinical observation, Rank found what he felt was a significant correlation between the easy birth and the well-adjusted individual on the one hand, and the difficult or painful birth and the anxiety-ridden and disturbed individual on the other. He reasoned that the first experience of the human individual in an independent existence was the event of birth. Although the event might not be remembered consciously, the marks of the event were deeply impressed on the physical and emotional life of the infant. The painful first experience in life tended to make the growing infant enter into each new experience with apprehension and dread. And according to Rank, those who were born of Caesarian section, with little or no discomfort, and no typical birth experience, moved easily into new events in life free of the emotionally defensive stance.

Whether we accept the full implication of Rank's birth trauma theory, we cannot easily escape the fact that the nature of the birth experience may have a profound effect upon the life of an individual. If such an early experience can so affect the concept of selfhood, it is not difficult to see that other powerful emotional experiences of early childhood can have a significant bearing on how the person meets life.

Nandor Fodor, a Hungarian psychoanalyst, has carried the theoretical process one step further backward, by suggesting that the psychic communication between the unborn infant and his mother is a major factor in creating the self-image and its constituent body image. If the mother resented the conception and hated the unborn child, the fetal being had no protection against such hatred, and was born with a backlog of self-disdain and other manifestations of low self-regard. If, on the other hand, the child was desired, planned for, and deeply loved in anticipation and in fact, this too would show in the feelings of self-acceptance and self-regard that shaped the emotional life of the individual.

Again, we do not need to accept the full implication of Fodor's theories to have a new sensitivity to the forces at work at the earliest moments in the life of the individual that shape the feeling about the self and the body within which the self dwells.

Some psychologists consider accidents to be forms of meaningful behavior. The unconscious drives toward self-injury make it a simple fact that a major portion of accidents happen to a small minority of people. A faulty body image and an urge to injure the self may well explain more of the self-destructive behavior that we observe than we are aware of.

We have looked at the two questions we raised at the beginning of this study: how does one develop a body image? and how does the healthy or unhealthy body image enrich or impair the ability of the individual to cope with life experience? We have come now to the nub of the issue. How does the body image reveal itself in the way an individual meets and moves through the experience of acute grief?

III.

The basic feeling that one has for his own body is acquired at such an early stage in the development of the personality that it is not usually subject to rational interpretation. It is made up of deep feelings that emerge from the reservoir of preconscious, subconscious, and unconscious experience. Therefore our understanding of it must take into account those forms of behavior that do not appear to be reasonable or rational. But we do not discount those feelings, for we have learned that all behavior is meaningful, and when it does not at all appear to be so, we are merely invited to look more deeply and carefully for that meaning.

Because the experience of death brings us face to face with the deepest emotions of life, much of the behavior we observe at such times has to be probed deeply for adequate understanding. In fact, some observed behavior involves compensations so powerful that the things we see mean quite the opposite from what we would at first assume.

Perhaps the point at which we can understand the dynamics of this process initially is not on the occasion of total death but with the experience of partial death. This is related most often to what is called the "phantom limb theory." When a soldier is severely wounded and must have a leg amputated, he experiences what is called the phantom limb response. I have interviewed many men in emergency military hospitals and have found that they tend to complain of acute pain in the nonexistent leg. The process that seems to be at work is that the complicated nerve center that had for a long time controlled the activity of the leg still continued to function. The body cannot at once divest itself of the activities and sensations that related it to one of its parts, now missing. It cannot at once relate itself to the new reality of the body image, and thus must engage in a rather lengthy withdrawal of sensation until the body image conforms to the body reality.

Marianne L. Simmel of Brandeis University has made a careful study of this phantom limb phenomenon.[1] She confirmed the theory that the body image develops slowly over long periods of time, but that it also tends to be more dependent upon past experience than present reality for its function. When she interviewed twenty-seven persons who had been born with a limb missing, she found no evidence of this phantom phenomenon. Also, in eighteen patients with leprosy, where a portion of body has wasted slowly away, the body image had a chance to conform to the body reality and there was no phantom sensation. She also found that it is the accumulation of experience which tends to fortify the phantom sensation, so that amputations in young children did not produce as much of this phenomenon as when the limb had been used enough to become a significant part of the total body experience. Her conclusion was that it is not simply the previous existence of the limb, but the memory of sensations associated with it, that make it a persistent part of the body image. Eventually the body image does conform to reality, but this takes time.

It has long been realized that the experience of grief has many of the characteristics of an amputation. In my book, *Understanding Grief*, I wrote, "Bereavement is an amputation of a part of the emotional structure of life, and the use of tears may help to wash away the separation." Just as the feelings may have difficulty at first in relating the fact of the body sensation with the modified body image,

---

1. Marianne L. Simmel, The Body Percept in Physical Medicine and Rehabilitation. Journal of Health and Social Behavior 8:60, 1967.

so the person who suffers acute loss may at first be so involved emotionally that it is difficult or impossible to separate the body image of the living being from the sensation of the death of the body in the lost object. Much of the feeling of pain that comes with the onset of acute grief is the feeling of emotional death. Although one cannot easily imagine his own death intellectually, he can be so identified with a love object that in its death he feels a loss of his life.

Basically, the grief process and the work of mourning are the effort of the living being to reorganize his damaged self-image and body image so that he can begin to function in terms of reality rather than in terms of the over-identification that now has no base in reality.

As the phantom limb experience is the experience of loss in part, so a study of the response to it can help us understand what takes place in total loss through death, and what can be done to aid the process of adjustment.

One thing we can be sure of is that there are wide variations in response to the experience of loss. Instant loss evokes far different feelings from gradual loss. The person who has been subject to a series of operations which removed each time more of the same limb has a different response from those who have met with sudden or accidental amputation. Thus, it would seem that the emotional responses of the bereaved after witnessing a long and obviously terminal illness are quite different from those who have been faced with tragic and untimely death.

The process of meeting the emotional crisis of death can be eased by wise procedures or it can be complicated by unwise attitudes and practices.

When a person or a culture is threatened irrationally by death it may develop the attitude of "hating the body of death." This hatred tends to make people do and say the things that will avoid an open and honest confrontation with death. Anxiety about death and fear of facing it honestly lead to practices which quickly and unceremoniously dispose of the dead. This in effect compounds the anxiety for it further restricts the process by which the body image of the living is disengaged from the body image of the dead. In their desire to get rid of the feared body of death, people tend to bind themselves to it permanently. It is only as death is faced and the reality of the death of the deceased is affirmed, that the life of the living is free to engage in the healthful process of withdrawal.

The inverse of this, of course, is the process by which love and respect for the unfeared body of death is expressed. Society has traditionally developed and each community has provided the ritualized events and ceremonial activities that make it possible for persons to act out their feelings of withdrawal of the body image of the living from the body identification with the dead. The funeral, with a healthful setting for the facing of the fact of physical death and the expression of the valid feelings related to the event, may well be the richest resource we have for protecting the body image of the bereaved individual from injury at the same time that it provides the community with a chance to do the kind of anticipatory grief work that reduces the acute hazard, and also provides an accepting climate for doing the unfinished work of mourning.

Unwise resolution of the threat of the death of those with whom strong identification exists may well lead to those feelings of self-damage and self-rejection that eventuate in accidents, suicide, depression, or neurotic behavior.

Wise resolution of the same emotional crises may strengthen the personality as it clarifies the self-image, and one learns to cope with crises more soundly. When this happens, the base for sympathy and empathy is strengthened, and the boundaries of selfhood are clarified. The phantom of unresolved grief with its persistent pain and its disorganization of life is bound up with unconscious and often irrational emotions that cannot be dealt with wisely unless we realize that their roots are in those labyrinths of consciousness that are not handled by rationalizations, intellectualized processes, or efforts at escape. Rather, we need to understand and protect the wise and sound processes by which the emotionally injured being is aided in coping with discomfort, in wisely acting out the feelings that cannot be put into words, and moving away from the damaging physical event with a restored strength for the body image and the identification of the healthful self-image.

UNDERSTANDING THE TEENAGER'S RESPONSE TO DEATH

Edgar N. Jackson

There was a time when it was assumed that adolescence was the best part of life. The teen-ager was considered to be free of the obligations of maturity and yet mature enough to enjoy life and its pleasures. Now these assumptions have been largely abandoned. Much of the evidence shows that the period from the end of childhood to the beginning of adulthood is filled with social, psychological, and emotional stress, and that our youth are having serious difficulties in moving through this period of life.

Part of the problem, at least, emerges at the point where the young face the meaning of life and death; when they try to come to terms with their own existence. Contemporary youth, born since the end of World War II, have been the first generation to feel the full brunt of the death-denying, death-defying concept of life that modern man adopted to help him escape the brutality, the suffering, and the death-centeredness of the war-time period. The implication was that if we denied war, it might go away, and if we did not face the meaning of nuclear devices, their destructiveness might never never be unleashed upon us. No matter how irrational and fanciful such attitudes may be, there has been little restraint on such modes of thought, and the group chiefly affected is our young people who have never known any other way of thinking.

Certainly, one aspect of what Geoffrey Gorer calls the "pornography of death" has been especially directed toward our children and youth. The flooding of the minds of children and youth with the comic-book version of brutality, sadism and apparently meaningless killing has long been a matter of concern. Frederic Wertham's book *Seduction of the Innocent* has made people aware of the problem of this type of informal and indiscreet education. But few seem to realize that this is but a part of the larger pattern of our culture that treats both life and death as trivial, without depth or purpose, and, at best, as intrusions on the thrills and sensational pursuits of the moment.

An unrealistic approach to death can be a hazard to adolescents as they face the major and significant tasks of this period of their lives.

147

In a recent book Avery Weisman, writing on the relation of responsibility to the sense of reality, says quite emphatically, "In short, to be responsible, man must believe in his own death." How difficult it is, then, for our teenagers to develop this form of responsibility, when the culture in which they are growing up works so hard to deny it.

This difficulty shows up at three points. The youth in any culture is faced with three major decisions: He is expected to lay the foundations for a philosophy of life; he is faced with the tasks of sexual adjustment that lead to the choice of a life partner; and he is expected to choose a vocation. In some cultures there is enough social structure to aid in making these choices, but in ours it is a complicated process with few fixed points of reference. It can be shown that the person's attitude toward death may in many cases be a significant factor in determining behavior in relation to these major choices.

Because a philosophy of life is basic to vocational choice and marriage attitudes, let us look at this first. The philosophy of life one develops may vary from time to time in response to one's life experience. Yet the meaning of life to the individual who is living it is a basic ingredient. And the meaning for the individual life is related to the attitudes toward life and death that are prevalent in the social context. The youth growing up in any given era is bound to be affected by that era, for good or ill.

The generation of youth now struggling to create a philosophy of life must contend with contemporary sources of anxiety, the prevalent concept of the future, and the impact of a death-denying, death-defying culture. While it is almost universal for teenagers to express some of their feelings for independence in revolt against their parents, adults like to feel that the future is in the hands of oncoming generations and that they can in some measure control it by their guidance. But in our time, youth is increasingly excluded from an orderly approach to the future, and the value structure that many adults live by seems to be seriously threatened by a whole generation of youth who see life and the world quite differently. Why is this so?

The teenager in our culture is largely a misfit. He has no active social function and no significant economic life. He is ostensibly preparing for a future that he does not define and is spending money that he does not earn. There are few jobs for teenagers, and our culture, with so much learning to transmit, must keep him in school for a long period of time. Even when he has finished his schooling, his future is uncertain because of the military needs of his society. All of this external experience is organized within a highly sensitive and carefully trained individual who draws his own philosophical conclusions. Often this leads him to a feeling of meaninglessness for the processes of life in which he is engaged, and causes him to face the future with apprehension and the present with various types of revolt.

Because the future is always related to concepts of life and death, he takes the anxiety that he has been steeped in, and the meaninglessness of the future which he has developed, and builds types of behavior that are expressions of both. He tends to focus his attention more and more on the present and on the satisfaction of his immediate needs. Increasingly, this becomes gratification without relatedness. As Gorer has shown, this leads to a breakdown of those refined capacities for genuine relationship that can bring meaning to life and that have always been the characteristics of the more truly mature and fulfilled human being.

These qualities of mind and emotion underlie the attitudes of youth toward death and dying. This process is surrounded by denials which make death something that only happens to other people. The emotions that are expressed at the breaking of relationships through death are apt to be of a foreign nature. This makes the traditional sentiments seem irrelevant and inappropriate. In their place are substituted games and other activities that show disregard for life, in an effort to show control over the anxiety about death. Such games as "chicken" illustrate this, as well as the suicidal activities examined in Abt's "Acting Out."

It is but a short step for the youth to direct his inherent idealism and his inherited apprehension toward the focal point of his anxiety. The meaninglessness of the future is equated with the meaninglessness of life and death. In this mood, anything that reminds him of the inevitable but threatening evidence of man's mortal nature is discredited or denied. Thus the significant therapeutic resources de-

149

veloped by society for meeting the emotional crises incident to death are apt to be ridiculed and destroyed.

On the other hand, these same forces at work in personality may become unconscious determinants in vocational choice. I have interviewed a large number of students in professional schools, and have had access to projective tests evaluating their emotional drives. I have found that in a significant number of instances the selection of a vocation was a form of behavior aimed at discovering answers about the meaning of life and death. This appeared to be especially true of clergymen, physicians, research psychologists, psychiatrists, and funeral directors. Perhaps this is one of the explanations for the dichotomy we see in modern society concerning death; the general community tends to ignore or deny the fact of death, whereas careful researchers in the field of human behavior give increasing consideration to the importance of death and a responsible approach to it as basic to maturity and to a sense of responsibility.

The same factors are at work in regard to the choice of a life partner. If the future is important and life perspectives are formed on the basis of an adequate philosophy of life, then marriage will be important and the selection of a partner will be seriously considered. On the other hand, if the future is nebulous and largely irrelevant to life, both the serious approach to the future and the ethical framework for such a future are discounted. This in turn leads to irresponsible sexual behavior and a further breakdown in the institution of marriage and the stability of the society of which it is an important part.

If we look carefully at the statistics on population, we see that today about half of the population in our country is 25 years of age or younger. This means that in our rapidly changing culture an increasingly large amount of the decision-making responsibilities will be in the hands of our youth. If they allow the prevalent patterns of culture to dominate their thinking and action, they will be increasingly death-denying and death-defying. But if they can be made aware of significant research findings on human behavior relating to death and a philosophy of life large enough to compass all of life experience, they will be responsive to those concerns which would adequately provide for the acute emotional crises of life, socially and psychologically.

It is quite obvious that the young people growing up in such rapidly changing times will not be satisfied with the answers of the past, which depended largely on tradition and unexamined premises. They will want to know why things are done as they are, what the values are in the old ways of doing things, and what the significance is for them in the rites, rituals, and ceremonials that they have inherited. That they will be responsive to answers to the personality sciences can be assumed, whereas they would show little response to the appeals of tradition and sentiment.

These young people will have grown up in the most affluent society in human history. They have been so saturated with things, that acquisition in and of itself does not impress them as much as it did their parents. They are more interested in services. They spend more and more on recreation, personal satisfaction, and their needs as individuals. Appeals on the basis of things like quality merchandise will make little response, but satisfactions on the basis of personal services will be valued. Thus, if the significant resources of our culture for meeting emotional crises are to be preserved during this era of rapid change, it will be done through an appeal to the values of those who represent the future. The values of our youth grow from a concern about their inner being, their feelings, and their apprehensions. If they can be understood and met at the level where they make their judgments, they can preserve the practices of the present for even more significant reasons than the present generation employs. If, however, the therapeutic resources which have been developed through the centuries to sustain life in crises are not interpreted to our youth primarily in terms of sentiment and tradition, material value, and social custom, they will be summarily rejected.

Whether we can move into the future with strengthened concepts of family living, significant motivations for vocation, and responsible and mature philosophies of life, may depend more than we realize on facing the personal and social problems that emerge at a point where we make it possible for our youth to confront the relevance of life to death, and of death to life.

REFERENCES FOR FURTHER READING

Erik Erikson, *The Challenge of Youth*, Doubleday Anchor

Edgar Z. Friedenberg, *Coming of Age in America*, A Vintage Book

Paul Goodman, *Growing Up Absurd*, A Vintage Book

Martha Wolfenstein, *Children and the Death of a President*, Doubleday

Douvan and Adelson, *The Adolescent Experience*, John Wiley and Sons

Erik Erikson, *Insight and Responsibility*, Norton

Frank, *Your Adolescent at Home and in School*, Viking

Peter Blos, *On Adolescence*, Free Press

Abt and Weissman, *Acting Out*, Grune and Stratton

Avery Weisman, *The Existential Core of Psychoanalysis*, Little Brown

Geoffrey Gorer, *Death, Grief and Mourning*, Doubleday

Erik Erikson, *Childhood and Society*, Norton

ALONENESS

Vincent Paris Fish

When death brings to an end the intimate companionship of man and wife, there occurs a traumatic severing of the most meaningful and sacred communication either has known. The immediate result is often withdrawal from all forms of communication with family, friends, and neighbors. In some instances, there is a cutting off of all communication with God, and church or synagogue. With the well-adjusted person, the severing of communication is temporary, and usually brief. But because, in a real sense, the surviving partner is no longer a complete being, all relationships with family and community are somehow changed, and a period of readjustment must be faced.

In order to understand the reasons why human beings react as they do to the death of a spouse or other loved one, we must seek the answers in an understanding of ourselves, particularly of our created needs for communication and companionship.

God created them male and female. God said, 'It is not good that man should be alone. I will make a helpmate for him. Therefore shall a man leave his father and mother, and shall cleave unto his wife: and they shall be one flesh'.

Thus Holy Scripture points out the elemental fact that man is a social animal. God created him that way. The smallest social unit is that of man and wife. God said that in marriage a man and wife become *one flesh*. St. Paul amplified this when he said, "He that loveth his wife loveth himself, for no man ever hated his own flesh." This principle is carried over into civil law in those cases where the testimony of one spouse might endanger the life of the other, as in a trial for murder. Society thus recognizes the *oneness* of the married state.

Death of a spouse, then, is indeed a traumatic experience. *Bereaved* means *to be robbed of a life*. The surviving partner of a marriage has been robbed of his companion. No other human relationship offers the fulfillment and intimacy of marriage. Grief rejects all sub-

153

stitutes. Relatives and friends cannot understand why their ministrations fail to suffice; their efforts end in frustration.

At this point in the life of the bereaved one, certain dangers arise. There is the temptation, for instance, to become anti-social, to become introspective and self-pitying. The result can well be self-destruction: mental, moral, spiritual, and sometimes physical. Another danger is to become so dependent upon relatives and friends that one is incapable of making decisions. This state of helplessness can become quite unbearable for all concerned. There is also the danger of projecting the period of mourning beyond all reason, with the result that the memory of the deceased becomes distorted in the mind of the one who mourns, through gross exaggeration of virtues or defects.

The loss of desire for proper food and nourishment is frequently a symptom of these dangers. Since the word companion means *one with whom we break bread*, it is logical that having lost that person, the taking of food has an unfortunate emotional impact upon the surviving mate. The breaking of bread is social, communal. Aloneness is not the proper climate for the partaking of food.

It is quite clear that the greatest service which can be done to aid the individual in adjusting to a whole new relationship with his fellow human beings is to encourage him to communicate his feelings to his pastor (priest, minister, rabbi), relatives, friends and neighbors. The natural compulsion to communicate should not be allowed to stifle under the mistaken notion that one's grief is purely private in nature. All human experiences are social. While it is true that some persons have been brought up to believe that disclosing their feelings is a sign of weakness and lack of breeding, the need to communicate is a desperate and natural one. The cutting off of such communication can bring about serious consequences. Furthermore, the beneficial results of communication of feelings of grief and fear cannot be overestimated. There is a purifying and alleviation of emotions and fears. Such a catharsis lessens the danger of psychological complexes. Not until the one who mourns has been emptied of all that troubles him, can the process of readjustment begin.

Through communication with listeners who are wise, as well as sympathetic, the one who mourns may find himself in touch with the most secure companionship of all. To understand that one is never really alone is of vast importance to all human beings, particularly to those trying to adjust to a new life without a mate. Belief in God, in His love for each soul, in His ever-present concern, is strengthening.

He that keepeth Israel neither slumbers nor sleeps. The hour has now come when each of you will go to your own tasks, and leave me alone. But I am not alone, because the Father is with me. Let not your heart be troubled . . . I go to prepare a place for you . . . that where I am, you may be also.

Through companionship with God, belief becomes reality. The fact that after death there is life, in the presence of God, becomes truth, not merely a tenet enunciated by Judaism and Christianity.

The religious person has a great reservoir of spiritual strength upon which to depend. Yet even to the devout, the role of priest, minister, or rabbi is crucial in the period of adjustment to bereavement. In those instances where there has been no religious background, or where the individual has fallen away from the church or synagogue, a greater difficulty presents itself in the matter of comforting or strengthening that person. When the clergyman is called upon for help, he will undoubtedly have feelings of guilt and strangeness to contend with, in addition to the normal emotions. It requires consummate skill to be of real assistance in such a situation. Yet in the time of grief, the heart is open to any sort of basic religious truth that is presented with sincerity and conviction.

The emphasis so far has been on the loss of a mate. Yet the loss of any loved one causes the same feelings of emptiness and aloneness. The same kind of readjustment to life must be made. It is important that all who suffer a loss remember that each human being has the same needs and longings, whether he be rich or poor, intellectually endowed or poorly educated.

By his very nature, man must communicate. This is especially true when trouble, sorrow and grief overtake him. Beneath the façade of every human being there is kindness and generosity waiting for those who will accept it. Sometimes the roughest exterior covers the softest heart. Just as the one who mourns needs help desperately, so do many human beings need desperately to provide that help; for communication of our thoughts and feelings is essential to every man's well-being.

Communication is even more vital when a man is overwhelmed by tragedy. He should not feel ashamed of this compulsion to communicate. God intends that he should communicate. Not to do so invites spiritual and physical disaster. Once he realizes the necessity to communicate, God expects him to take the initial steps in opening the lines of communication in order to accept the overtures of love, and friendship, and pastoral care that are made available.

In the Book of Ecclesiastes, we find these words:

> To everything there is a season, and a time to every purpose under the Heaven: A time to be born, and a time to die; a time to plant, and a time to harvest; a time to weep, and a time to laugh; a time to mourn, and a time to dance; a time to keep silence, and a time to speak.

Each soul has a purpose in God's plan. It is the nature of that soul to pursue the life He has given it and to fulfill its purpose. No man is alone. Every man must share all aspects of the common lot. Aloneness is a mirage rising up from the desert of grief, and tragedy, and frustration. But the waters of compassion are as near as the human heart; they will refresh and strengthen any man who reaches forth in love and trust. As soon as possible, the person who mourns should seek the waters of comfort within the hearts and souls of fellow human beings. This is the time for them to speak.

ENFORCED INTIMACY AND BEREAVEMENT

FREDERICK D. HAYES

(From the point of view of a minister in a small city)

As a theological student, I served a small crossroad church. When, after graduation, I went to minister in a larger community, the county seat, a professor who taught courses in a subject known as "Rural Church" wrote to me and asked what changes I had made in my preaching. Rather rashly, I answered, "None. People are people." That answer has some merit, but I would answer somewhat differently today, for I have learned that the environment does play a very real part in the reactions of people to problems that are common to all, regardless of where they may live.

The small New England city where I have ministered for twenty-four years has a population of about 24,500. Situated across the river is a sister city with a population of 40,800. These two cities are thirty miles from the next large city. Consequently, together they form a closely knit unit in all their interests. This is important because it brings us to the very point with which I wish to deal, and it has direct bearing on helping or hindering one in making a recovery from grief.

When one faces bereavement and all that goes with it in a small city, he is faced with both the positive advantages and the negative aspects of what some sociologists have called enforced intimacy. A death in the small community inevitably touches more people with whom the bereaved is associated. Certain relationships have been changed for a larger number of people in this community than, I suspect, is true in a community of greater size. More *people who live* within a short distance of the bereaved, who earn their living working near him, who belong to the same church, who have joined the same clubs, who go to the same theaters, who shop at the same stores, and so on, are aware of the death in the family.

People in a small city are more closely bound together and I think more aware not only of the changes death brings but of the presence of the bereaved in their midst.

Here is an illustration of this fact: My mother died just a few weeks after I moved to this community. As early spring weather in this climate makes it almost impossible to keep a car clean for more than a few hours, on the morning of the funeral I drove into a filling station where cars were washed. I had never traded at this station. I did not know any of the attendants by name, hardly by sight. None of them were members of my parish. Immediately, one of the attendants said, "Leave your car here. We will wash it and deliver it to your home right away." Another said, "Come, I'll take you to your house now. You must have your hands full today." That experience made me feel that I was not alone; that others, unknown to me, had the quality of understanding and the desire to help. The fact that I was a minister in the community probably helped in making me known to the men at the filling station more quickly than otherwise, but this type of response is not unusual because, in general, people in a small community are cognizant of what is happening in the daily lives of their neighbors. This knowledge can be a source of comfort and strength in an hour of bereavement.

During the Second World War, an Army officer in another small city with which I am familiar, who had just returned from the area of conflict, had been invited to speak at the noonday luncheon of the local Service Club. I overheard two of the club members speaking of the fact that this would be the first meeting that another one of the members had attended since learning that his son had been killed in action. These men were concerned that the Army officer might possibly say something about his war experiences which would make it unnecessarily difficult for the bereaved father. When the speaker arrived, they quietly took him aside and informed him of the situation.

This communal concern and intimacy enters into the total picture at the time of a death in the family. The mortician may be your table companion at the Rotary Club, you may have played bridge with the Judge of Probate every month for years, the florist who arranges the flowers for the funeral is on a degree team with you at the lodge, the doctor who cared for your dear one lives on the next street, the nurse who was so kind-hearted at the hospital sits two pews from you at church, the caretaker at the cemetery is on your bowling team at the Y.M.C.A., and the insurance man's young son plays in the Little League with your own. You will be meeting these same people day after day as you go through the experience of coming to terms with the fact that death has come to one dear to you. Every meeting will bring thoughts to your mind concerning the experiences of the immediate past, and also thoughts that go back beyond the immediate past to other days and other experiences. The past comes back rather easily to one who lives in a small community. He lives with it.

Personalities are different and the way each one reacts to this enforced intimacy will be conditioned by many factors: religious faith, temperament, cultural background, health, the length and severeness of the sickness that preceded the death, etc., etc. A very important factor is concerned with the survivors in the immediate family and how near or far away they live. This applies not only to their geographical but to their psychological remoteness or nearness as well. Countless other factors enter into the way in which one meets the problems of overcoming a grief which threatens to be self-defeating and excessive. In the small community, it is much harder to "forget" the preciousness of the relationship that death has tried to shatter; but victory over grief does not come by attempting to forget. Healing comes to the person who is able to see that whatever the dead person has stood for in all the relationships of his life is still a part of his ongoing life. The poet was not talking nonsense when he wrote: "It is given to love to keep its own eternally." The small community can be a very vital factor in helping one come to this realization. Considerable force of will may be required to face up to the fact of bereavement and to comprehend that life lived with the dead one is still going on—changed, of course, but ever present. The intimacy of a small community can reinforce this necessary act of will. Immediately after the bereavement, it will be more difficult for people of certain temperaments to make necessary adjustments. One may happen to have what is known as the New England temperament:

> "To love so fiercely that the hand trembles,
>   that the deep eyes ache,
>   Yet speak of love infrequently, and tersely."

This type of person may insist on no display of emotion and, in fact, may seek to avoid the mention of his loss. But, living in a small town, he is going to meet people daily in the total life of the community who feel they must say something about his loss when they meet him for the first time after the event. Some will handle the situation with grace and tact; others, just as well-meaning and sincere, may be quite clumsy and even provoke a new state of mental anguish. This applies of course everywhere, but in a small community these occasions are apt to be more frequent and continue over a longer period of time. Many times I have had a parishioner say to me, "One of the hardest things I have had to face was to go down the street the first few times." ("Down the street" in a small town refers to the business section.)

I suppose it boils down to the fact that the individual has to go on living in the same community and meeting the same people, again and again, who have been so intimate a part of both his life and the dear one's. And yet, in the small town, more people are conscious that a deep loss has been suffered than they would be in a greater city or area.

One has to go on living in the home where the bereavement has taken place. One has to go on living in the same rooms once shared with the departed, sit in the same chairs, look at the same pictures, and so on. Fortunate is the man who can accept the reality of this situation without closing off certain rooms, removing pictures from the walls, avoiding certain furniture. Slowly, at first, but then more quickly, as time ministers to grief, one comes face to face with a *deeper* reality, namely, that the life which has been shared still goes on, that the one who has passed from physical sight and existence is still a part of our life. The old familiar things can help, not hinder, our realization of this.

Similarly, the enforced intimacy of the small city can be, and often is, of very real help in enabling us to grasp this truth and to lay hold of its healing powers.

HELPING CHILDREN COPE WITH DEATH

Edgar N. Jackson

Death is a part of natural order. The casual observer can see it all around in plant and animal life. But underlying death there is another order, the phenomenon of ever-renewed life. For the individual, death in general does not usually present the problem that a specific death produces. To a parent, one of the more difficult educational tasks is that of helping a child to develop the insight and the resources to cope with the specific death that becomes a part of his experience.

To help a child take a healthful approach to the fact of death, the first thing that an adult must do is to come to terms with his own fears and feelings on the subject. The barrier to communication is usually more emotional than verbal. When he has sorted out his own feelings, he feels freer to talk without restraint to the child who comes to him laden with questions.

When should you talk to a child about death? Usually a child will show his interest in the subject directly. It may appear in playing hospital, in playing war, or in playing with toy guns. His games are explorative behavior to see how he feels about ideas. Or he may make comments and ask questions that show he is thinking about the subject. Some event in the family, in the neighborhood, or in the news may precipitate the question. It may be filled with emotion or merely with curiosity. But most often the child raises the question of death when his interest or experience is confronted by it.

What kinds of questions do children ask? Usually they are closely related to experience. They may include imagination or show the emotional climate that surrounds the experience. But usually they are simple and direct efforts to satisfy curiosity and gain information. The question should be answered in the mood in which it is asked. If the child seeks simple information and is greeted with an avalanche of emotion, he will have difficulty relating the answer to the question. For him it may seem unanswered, and the anxiety related to the asking of it will remain.

That is the time for answers. Evasion creates apprehension. This starts the process of adding an unwarranted emotional dimension to the simple question, and may make it difficult or impossible to ask more. The simple and direct answer dispels anxiety and gives confidence that the subject is not taboo and can be explored.

One of the hazards most adults encounter in these situations is their own tendency to overanswer. They complicate the problem by trying to answer their own questions rather than by adhering only to the question the child asks. It is better to ask the child questions that can sharpen and clarify his interest rather than to overanswer. Just asking "How do you mean?" or, if the question is quite general, "Just what was it you wanted to know?" may be all that is needed to clarify matters. Often the adult's apprehension about death adds much more to the question than the child had in mind. Overanswering may well be the indication of anxiety, and the child is far more responsive to the anxiety than he is to the complicated answer.

What should you tell a child about death? The answer to this question is related to the age of the child, the nature of the event, and the degree of his interest in it. He may be flooded inside with questions. These indicate the growing depth of his thought and feeling. He should be made to feel comfortable in his asking. He should be made to feel that the fact of death can be dealt with competently by people around him. While he may well be aware of the emotional content of the experience—for those around him may not be able to hide their feelings—he also should feel that they are not helpless facing the event.

Honest answers are important to a child. Children have a built-in lie detector; a child senses it when he is not getting a truthful answer. This tends to compound his anxiety, for then, not only is he not getting the answers he needs, but also he is finding some emotions he does not need. He feels insecure with adults who are afraid of his questions. He feels threatened by the feeling that his communication with others has broken down. He may not know how to explain it, but when he has more questions, he may not want to ask them of an unsatisfactory source, and thereupon he withdraws into his own thoughts or looks elsewhere for answers.

Young children have no sense of time or distance. The house on the corner seems a long way off. The now is important, and a day or a week or a month are indistinguishable. The approach to life is largely emotional. When an important person is gone from that life, it is important to fill in the blank spot with emotional warmth and added security until the child adapts to the differences. For an older child, curiosity may be added to the feeling of deprivation, and he may ask questions that show he is trying to understand what death is like physically. He wants to clarify his understanding of how death is different from life. Or he may ask questions that show he wants to know what difference death makes in the variety of human relations.

The teenager, filled with a new sense of the creative power of life and the wonder of the future, shows his interest in the subect by a quest for the spiritual, psychological, and personal meanings of death. He is busily engaged in welding his philosophy of life and needs to have a place into which death will fit. The teenager who is most apt to need special help is the one who cannot talk about death when it occurs. He is probably indicating that he cannot cope with the idea, and his *philosophy of life is not big enough* to find a place for it.

Children and young people are a help to the adults around them in encouraging an open and honest discussion of events. Their questions are apt to be direct and forthright. This makes it easier for the adult to come to terms with his own thoughts and feelings at the same time that he is trying to understand and answer properly the queries of the child.

Often questions are raised as to the participation of children in funerals and the other ceremonial events that surround death. We need to recognize that the funeral is not merely the religious service, but is also all of the events from the time of death through the interment, in which the religious and social community participates. It involves the planning, the visitations, the coming together of the family and the emotional support of the neighbors. Naturally, the child knows that something unusual is going on and he wants to be a part of it. While he may not know the fuller meaning of the events, he does want to participate to the extent that he can understand them. While it would never be wise to force a child to do things he finds threatening or unacceptable, he should be made comfortable in participating in the event up to the limits of his ability. He can understand his inclusion far better than he can understand his exclusion. If he is old enough to go to church, he is old enough to go to a funeral. If he is curious about what goes on at the funeral home, it would be better to satisfy his curiosity rather than to surround it with an emptiness that his imagination would fill. In addition, it might be helpful to take the child to the funeral home when there are few people around and no service is in progress, so that his questions can be answered freely. In this way, he meets the event openly and honestly. The anxiety is reduced at the same time that his understanding increases.

Basically, a child should be helped to see that natural death is not tragic. Although it brings changes to life, that life is supported by a faith that man's spirit is not obliterated by anything incidental to his physical nature. However, he should be taught from the circumstances surrounding unnatural and untimely death that man has responsibilities toward himself and others. In order to live the full and abundant life, he must avoid behavior that is careless, sinful, and ignorant both in himself and in others.

When this is done, death is not separated from life and man's responsibility. He does not then blame God for what is the unwise action of men. Rather, death becomes a significant event in the personal history of all mortal creatures that must ultimately be faced. The way of life that lives always as if it were aware of this fact tends to be more spiritually mature and morally conscious. So, in truth, we can learn much about the facts of life from the facts of death. Then, and perhaps only then, does our religious faith become fully relevant, for it is a faith that does not shun death, but makes even of this event a time for witness and an evidence of faith in those qualities of being that survive physical dissolution.

E. PRACTICAL MINISTRY AND CARE

COUNSEL FROM A DOCTOR WHO IS A MINISTER

WILLIAM B. McCULLOUGH

I have, both as a minister and a physician, talked with those who have lost a loved one. There is no doubt but that the person of faith is best equipped to deal with his loss. Many discover an equanimity that they never knew they possessed. At the same time, it is the genuinely religious person who finds special problems. Perhaps he expects more from life and death. Usually he is more introspective. Frequently he is expected to be a source of strength for others at the same time he is himself deeply grieved.

I have observed again and again that the strength one has at the time of bereavement is based on the faith one has developed over years. It is rare that a person discovers a faith during the period of grief that he did not have before. It is also rare that the man of faith fails to find that the God in whom he believes offers him more than he had expected. The bereaved does not need to be told of the value of his faith at the time of death. He has experienced it and knows in his deepest self the "comforting hand of God." The purpose of this chapter is to discuss some of the conflicts that many face at the time of bereavement. It is based on the belief that many experiences that are new to the individual are common to mankind, and in times of crisis, the bereaved will be able to draw upon the discoveries of others to enable him to grieve deeply, and to emerge with a better understanding of himself, his world and his God.

The initial shock of the sudden death of a loved one brings a kind of paralysis. One is without direction or feeling. This paralysis gradually changes to disbelief or denial—"It isn't so." "It can't be true." But eventually disbelief gives way to a developing awareness of the loss. This transition may take hours or days. It is usually a matter of days that the full impact of what has happened slowly settles into full consciousness.

The funeral or memorial service usually takes place in the midst of the developing awareness of loss. Friends and relatives, by sharing grief or by their concern, provide comfort for the bereaved. The service itself is also a symbolic sharing with the deceased in his death. The funeral represents to many a contact with a source of strength beyond their own. The presence of God is for many believers a deep and genuine reality. God is not questioned or analyzed here, but His Presence is experienced. It is felt as courage, and one is grateful. It is felt as strength; one knows with the Psalmist that even in the "valley of the shadow of death . . . Thou are there."

But some fail to find solace in their services. For this they should not chastise themselves. Such a lack of significance may be a part of the normal human reactions of numbness and withdrawal in the face of loss.

It is usually after the funeral that the full impact of the death is realized. This is the beginning of the stage of mourning that requires active participation on the part of the bereaved. Up to this time events have been thrust upon the bereaved. Now begins the time of restitution or "grief work." Comfort, which up to this point, has been so important, is now not enough; one must accept the pain of bereavement. This is a time of paradox; the memories of the deceased are both sweet and painful; the future is frightening and challenging. For most people the task cannot be undertaken alone. It is essential that the bereaved have someone with whom he can talk—someone who will be able to listen. A sympathetic friend who is filled with advice but unable to be silent and listen will not do. The listener may be a friend or relative who shares a special closeness with the bereaved, or who himself has experienced deep grief. It may be a clergyman or a psychiatrist or pastoral counselor who is able to listen. A word of caution must be said to the parent of older children who has lost a spouse. Although openness between parent and child is essential, one should seek another adult in whom to confide his deepest feelings. The child needs the parent as a confidant. The parent needs another adult.

There are some specific areas where conflicts are faced particularly by the religious person in these weeks of grief work and restitution. They include loneliness, guilt, asking why, and the future.

Loneliness and Solitude

Everyone who faces the death of a person whom he has loved feels profound loneliness. The loneliness is painful, not only because of the profound loss but because this loneliness touches the essential aloneness of man. For it is the destiny of man to be alone and to know that he is alone. It may well even be true in some way beyond the dimensions of time that death is the first introduction into an existence where one is not alone.

The word "loneliness" describes the pain of being alone. But there is also another word for being alone: "solitude." Solitude expresses the glory of being alone. The transition from loneliness to solitude is not clear cut; both states often exist side-by-side. It requires courage to face loneliness, to dare to be alone. It is the experience of many that to face the intensity of loneliness and its true pain is to change loneliness into solitude; the power of loneliness is destructive only when we run from it. To experience it fully is to change it into solitude. In solitude we come to meet ourselves as we truly are. It is in moments of solitude that something happens to us. The experience of the power of loneliness is at the heart of mourning. "Blessed are those who mourn, for they shall be comforted." [1]

Guilt

Frequently the bereaved is overwhelmed by a feeling of guilt. The possibility of rectifying past errors or of carrying out plans for a person is suddenly closed to us.

If his feelings of guilt persist the grief-stricken person should be encouraged to discuss them with his pastor or a professional counselor. But guilt is often resolved simply in learning that it is a common component of grief.

Our closest relationships are never perfect, and there is always some basis for guilt. The man of faith, however, will understand that his guilt will be forgiven. The highest love of man, like the love of God, accepts us as we are, demanding nothing of us but to be what we are. The experience of basic guilt and the grace of forgiveness were expressed most profoundly by the late Paul Tillich.

Grace strikes us when we are in great pain and restlessness. It strikes us when we walk through the dark valley of a meaningless

---

1. Matthew 5:4.

and empty life. It strikes us when we feel that our separation is deeper than usual . . . when, despair destroys all joy and courage. Sometimes at that moment a wave of light breaks into our darkness, and it is as though a voice were saying: "You are accepted. You are accepted, accepted by that which is greater than you, and the name of which you do not know. Do not try . . . to do anything now; perhaps later you will do much. Do not seek for anything; do not perform anything; do not intend anything. Simply accept the fact that you are accepted!" If that happens to us, we experience grace.[2]

Asking Why

There is no doubt that we cannot answer the personal "why" of the death of a child or a young man or woman or one "in the prime of life." To say "It is God's will" is satisfying only for a few of those with genuine faith. Our reasoning, even prayerful thought, reaches an impasse. Yet there is something within us which hammers at the closed door. Save for the aged, whose life "has been lived," death comes as a tragedy. The physician often turns off or tones down his feelings because he is confronted with death day after day. The clergyman, all too often feeling the need to provide an answer, misses the depth of the tragedy. Thus, the bereaved finds himself alone on the battlefield where tragedy and hope fight each other without victory.

The Psalmist can exclaim, "Precious in the sight of the Lord is the death of his saints."[3] The Psalms also abound in expressions of human despair, and unanswered questions. Perhaps the reason for the lack of answers is that every human way of thinking ultimately reaches embarrassment at every point. Perhaps the beginning of understanding is this human despair. Perhaps it is only at this point, standing empty-handed, that we can hear a voice from a dimension other than that in which we ordinarily live. Here, where reason has been exhausted, we can be open to a deeper and higher dimension of life.

---

2. Tillich, P.: "You are Accepted" in *The Shaking of the Foundations*, New York: Charles Scribner's Sons, 1948.

3. Psalm U6:15.

It is in despair that we meet faith as it comes to us "from without," faith as a gift.

The experience of many is that the acceptance of death as a tragedy which we cannot explain does not cast them into despair, but rather gives them new strength. In facing tragedy, something happens to them to give them meaning and a drive toward the future. One may call this revelation the presence of God, but what one calls this experience is of secondary importance. What is primarily important is the assurance that the helplessness of despair can be transcended. St. Paul expressed this, "O death, where is thy victory? O death, where is thy sting?" [4] The death and resurrection of which he speaks refers not only to that of the deceased but to that of the living. The bereaved has died to certain patterns and ways of living but may be resurrected through the comfort and hope proffered by others and by his religion. This is a gift, this is grace. This event is not a sudden experience. But gradually, often at first imperceptibly, the bereaved experiences renewed interest and direction, and realizes he has been granted the rewards of the work of mourning.

The Future

"Life goes on . . . I forget just why," Edna St. Vincent Millay wrote. It is from this point that the bereaved begins. A great part of the work of grief involves the sorrowful and joyous recalling of past memories, in thought, in discussions, even in dreams. It is to those who do this work of sifting memories and emotions that the future belongs. The desire to be with the deceased is eventually replaced by a desire to fulfill his finest aspirations and wishes. "Time heals all," *not in the sense of an anesthetic,* but in the use of the time of mourning to lead the bereaved to a new life and new relationships, enriched by a positive identification with the lost person. "We experience only what is built into our life, has become an element in it, and is surpassed by the drive toward the future; for life is the drive toward the future." [5] The work of grief leads us back into life.

---

4. I Corinthians 15:55.
5. Foss, M.: *Death, Sacrifice and Tragedy.* Lincoln, University of Nebraska Press, 1966.

We are changed, deepened, more able to offer solace to others, more able to live significantly and, in the best sense, joyously.

In the Gospel according to Matthew, Jesus invited a man to follow him. The man agreed, but said, "Let me first go and bury my father." Jesus replied, "Leave the dead to bury their own dead." [6] What first appears to be disrespect for the deceased and death itself is rather a profound respect for life and living to the fullest.

Some regard the prolongation of grief a spiritual duty. They could not be more mistaken. To gather oneself together and move on at the right time is an essential part of the truly religious life. Indeed it is only the genuinely religious man who can mourn, and then, out of the sadness and richness of his grief, enter fully into active life. The one who has felt loneliness and experienced its change to solitude, who has forgiven himself and accepted his anger and guilt, is the one whose weeping has made him free, and who, without answers to his "whys" is again able to enter fully into the living of each day. It is the result of his faith that he is able to be renewed. He can plan a meaningful future and enjoy rich human relationships. "Blessed are those who mourn, for they SHALL be comforted."

---

6. Matthew 8:21, 22.

THE CHALLENGE OF LIFE

ROBERT L. MILES

I recall the problem that I had as a medical student in accepting the death of patients in the hospital. I can still recall the first patient whom I saw die. She was an elderly lady who had suffered a stroke. There was no other avenue for her but that of death. Yet the knowledge that this woman was breathing her last was deeply disturbing to me.

As the son of a Methodist minister, I had been raised in an atmosphere in which God and Jesus Christ were a very real part of the household. Although some teachers in the church had taught that we should accept death as God's will, my father did not stick to the letter of this basic teaching. To him, life was composed of three basic parts: first was the coming of life, or birth; second was an indeterminate span, the actual living of life; third was the termination of life on earth, or death. He felt that this was God's will, and there is much in the Bible to substantiate that postulation. However, throughout life many events induced by men exert their influence on us. These cannot be blamed on God.

It is sometimes too easy for the physician to use God and fate as the scapegoat for his ignorance of life and death; or his willingness to sit down with the bereaved to discuss the factors concerning the demise of the loved one: or his lack of understanding of the survivor's needs. It is a fact that there are physicians who, lacking the "milk of human kindness," regard death as a part of everyday events. The doctor can accept it; why can't the family? If there are problems arising from grief, these are relegated to the ministerial function, not the medical.

During my internship, I learned to accept death as a reality. I was in charge of the hospital one night when an elderly patient was brought in. His death was expected, as he was in severe congestive heart failure. The attending physician told me to do what I could, but acknowledged that the condition was hopeless. The patient's wife urged me to save him if at all possible. I spent the rest of the night in the intensive care unit working on the patient. All of the necessary drugs, equipment, and personnel were at hand. By dawn we had done all that could be done. It had been an exhausting night, but the first rays of the new Sunday morning brought also a new ray of life for the patient. The battle had been won.

My fatigue vanished when I saw the husband and wife holding hands that morning and looking at each other with a love and understanding that came from fifty years of marriage. Two weeks later he was discharged from the hospital. I did not see the patient again for several weeks. I did hear from his attending physician that he was doing well and leading a normal life. He and his wife had fully realized the new lease on life that they had been given and were using it to the fullest advantage.

About eight months later, I was again on call when Gus was again brought in unconscious as an emergency case. This time we were faced with a severe stroke which had paralyzed him. This time there was no heroic therapy to be given. There was no life-saving drug regime to be used to fight the challenge of death. There was no chance for survival.

But this time something else was different. His wife did not plead for his life. She did not ask that we do all that we could to save him. She had had one gift of renewed life and was able to enjoy the extra months they had had together. This time she knew that survival would bring grief and suffering for him. She accepted the news of his death with a quiet calm that I have seen many times since, when the surviving spouse knows deep down that death relieved the loved one's suffering and that, in this instance, it was not something to be feared.

Shortly after Gus' death, I was called to the OB delivery room in a hurry. Two mothers were about to give birth. After I delivered the children, I hurried down to the newborn nursery to check the infants and see that all was well. I shall recall many times the look on the faces of the new parents as they viewed these small babes that they had produced and brought into the world.

It was then that I fully realized that this was the way of life. We are born, we live, and we die. It is this that is God's will. When one passes from this world to whatever is beyond (and I personally feel there is something beyond) new life comes to take the place of those who have had their experience on earth. From that time on, I had no problem accepting death. I have accepted its inevitability, but what about the others who have lost a loved one? How can my experiences help them to overcome their pain of loss or make their suffering any less?

You who read this must accept the fact that one must have faith. There must be a faith in a higher being than mortal man; faith in an Omnipotent Presence. There must be something more than mortal life upon earth. Man is capable of many great things and has scored many truly magnificent accomplishments in the fields of science, engineering, physics, and related areas. Yet, man cannot create life. Man can harness the energies of atomic power, and yet cannot create the simple violet which withstands the ravages of winter's storms and whose delicate beauty peeks through the cold barren crust of soil each spring. Man can grow food to feed millions of people, but only the bee can manufacture honey from the flower. Man can extend life, make it more pleasant and healthful, but he cannot prevent death. The fact of death is God's will.

To those of you who have faith, grief will be less bitter and less painful. Grief is a natural human characteristic. It is only natural that man should mourn one who had been close. But his grief should be tempered with the realization that only a physical essence is gone. That tangible vehicle we call the body had lost its function for whatever physical reason there might have been. The cancer that has eroded the vital areas and sapped the strength from the body can be blamed for this. Maybe it was the heart that had been damaged until it no longer beat and sent life-giving blood to the rest of the body. These are the physical factors which we must face. Surely we cannot blame them on God.

In fact there is no real reason to try to assess blame when death comes, in an attempt to soften the blow of loss. The same holds true in the case of an accidental death or one caused by a criminal act. To place the blame on a person or persons will not ease the grief of the survivors.

"If only I had . . . or had not . . ." How many times have those of us in the area of professional counseling heard this expression in connection with death? We try to fix the blame for the death of a loved one. Some feel that if we blame someone or something the grief will be eased. This is not so. Blaming someone is actually harder on people, since one day they must come to grips with the situation as it really is and the guilt feelings are often harder to overcome at this time than if they had been wrestled with at the time of the problem. To attempt to affix blame on someone or something in an attempt to modify grief is only a temporary measure to avoid the issue; it is a "crutch."

When we grieve, we grieve not for the dead but the living. Grief is not for the one who is gone but for those of us left behind. The challenge of death is for the living. The dead leave us a legacy of life still to be lived. To grieve is normal. To have feelings of guilt, hostility, fear, panic, and hopelessness is normal. But to give in to these emotions is not normal. The gift of life should not be squandered by excessive surrender to these feelings. They should be dealt with openly and truthfully. There should be no shame in admitting them. Frank, open discussion, no matter how difficult it might seem at the time, should be undertaken as soon as they appear. It is far better to meet emotions head on than to try to suppress them and let them grow until they cloud reason, good judgment, and common sense. Just a bit of wise counsel at the proper time will prevent more grief and suffering later on.

Life continues as a cycle and series of events; some good, and some bad. All are irreversible. What is done is done, and cannot be erased. Death is one of those factors of life. It, too, is irreversible, inevitable. Life has been described as the one incurable disease which afflicts all mankind. Some live only a few breaths of life and die. Each man is a person unto himself, subject to the whims and chances of heredity, self-abuse, and the multiple effects of environment. This is the closest that one can come to the "Why" of death.

We who are the living cannot expect to turn to the deceased for the forgiveness of our sins, the cleansing of our souls or the solace for our grief. We can, however, seek the strength for our living from them. Does this sound strange? Not at all.

Several years ago, a young mother who had been a patient of mine died in an accident. Her husband was left with three children, one to five years of age. When I told him the sad news of his wife's death, he wept openly, as one would expect. He then began to suffer the usual emotions, guilt that he had gone out that particular night, even though he had taken the children on a long-awaited outing; remorse for having stayed so late; and panic at the thought of "What will I do now?" In the stillness of the hospital at four o'clock in the morning, we sat together while I encouraged him to talk and vent his feelings. I then asked him, "What would your wife want you to do now? What would she want for your children? How would she advise you in this situation?" He responded to this idea at once. A new strength came to him in that moment. What had been utter despair in one moment became definite decision in the next. In the days that followed, he handled what was a very tragic and most difficult situation with a strength that he had not shown before his wife's death. Since that time, he has raised the children to be well-adjusted, healthy in mind and body. Although before his wife's death he had not really been a believer in God, he now found faith, and he has maintained it ever since. Strength to go on living came to him from the death of his lovely wife.

We must all look at death in a realistic manner. It cannot be ignored. It is final and yet it is not. The physical body is gone but the soul of man lives forever. We who survive must not fear death nor must we fear life. We must accept the challenge of life that is put to us by the death of a loved one. When there are children or other members of the family remaining, we must see to it that they do not suffer any more than is unavoidable. We cannot withdraw from the human race, even briefly, while we mourn excessively at our loss.

We must accept the challenge of death as a challenge to live. We must not lose from death but rather gain strength from the passing. Though we have lost the physical being of our loved one, we must realize that our life must go on to its natural conclusion. Since we do not know when that will be, we must live our lives to the fullest; we must take the avenues of living that are open to us and make the most of them.

This is the real victory that can come to those who have lost someone. It is in this manner that we do not really lose but gain from death. Socrates once said:

To fear death, gentlemen, is nothing other than to think oneself wise when one is not; for it is to think one knows what one does not know. No man knows whether death may not even turn out to be the greatest of blessings for a human being; and yet people fear it as if they knew for certain that it is the greatest of evils. Be of good hope in the face of death. Believe in this one truth for certain: that no evil can befall a good man either in life or death, and that his fate is not a matter of indifference to the gods.

A PASTORAL CALL FOLLOWING DEATH

EDGAR N. JACKSON

Abundant material growing from independent research in the personality sciences points up the importance of the care of the bereaved. Geoffrey Gorer, the English anthropologist, says that the two periods of life when persons are most in need of emotional support are during infancy and during the adjustment to acute loss through death.

Dr. Erich Lindemann writes that the most difficult period for most persons faced with adjustment to death comes not at the time of the death or the funeral, but rather at a time ten days to two weeks after the event. At this time friends and relatives have returned to their usual activities, and the grieving person is obliged to face the tasks of rebuilding his life framework now so damaged by death.

The pastor is in a position to minister to the emotional needs of these people by visiting in the home. He has been close to the family during the period of family activity as well as during community and religious ceremonials following the death. He is aware of thoughts and feelings in a way that is not easily shared by anyone else. He is in a position to give emotional support and spiritual guidance.

In the pastoral relationship described in the following, the pastor called at the home of Mrs. Lawrence, an active member of the parish, ten days following the funeral of her husband. Mr. Lawrence had died unexpectedly following minor surgery. He was sixty-three, five years older than his wife.

I found Mrs. Lawrence pensive and subdued. She was responsive but seemed to be deep in a mood of self-criticism. It was not hard to see that she was harboring guilt feelings, and that she was determined to question me about a conversation I had held with her husband in private during his hospital stay. Without violating his confidence, I was able to assure her that we had talked about theological interpretations of life and death. She had been so eager to ask, "Did he talk about me?" that I recognized her apprehension, and at my reply, "He didn't say anything about you during our conversation," she relaxed visibly. But then she went on to talk most volubly about how she and her husband had shared their thoughts and feelings, and into this discourse there crept a note of defensiveness. She was still in the grip of apprehension and feelings of guilt.

Finally she blurted out, "Do you think I helped to kill George?"

I said, "I don't think I know what you mean."

"Oh, it's a long story," she said, "But I can't help blaming myself. It's so hard to explain because it's so personal. But you understand such things, I suppose. I might as well tell you. It won't do any harm now and it might do some good, for maybe you could help me live with it."

She paused to look at me but I said nothing.

She continued, "You know we never had any children. The Lord knows we wanted them but we never had any. I don't know what the matter was. We weren't the kind to run to doctors with things like that. Years went by and we were still hoping and then, finally, we accepted the fact and didn't talk about it much. I knew George was disappointed, and I was, too. Whenever he was any place with children around he seemed to enjoy them so much, playing with them, you know, and watching them all the time. I could tell what he was thinking, but he never said anything. I always felt he was blaming me. He never said so, but I always had the feeling he was disappointed with me.

"Then one day he came home all excited about the chance to adopt a little boy. He had heard about it through a friend who was connected with an agency. It was all set, I guess. But I blew up. I guess I felt he was telling me what he thought of me. Anyway, I let him have it. I said that if we couldn't have any children of our own, I sure wasn't going to take on somebody else's. I said a lot more. I don't know yet why I exploded so, but I was so disappointed with things that this seemed the last blow. I yelled at him and said things I hate to remember. I was surprised at myself, for I am not usually that way. Even while I was doing it, I felt sorry but I couldn't stop. He was quiet through it all. He looked stunned, and I can still see him. He said he was sorry I took it that way, and we never said another word about it through all these years.

"I couldn't say I was sorry, and he seemed afraid to bring up the subject. It just went on and on. I kept thinking that maybe I would

180

say something, but I never did. I know he was disappointed with me. He still watched children as if he wanted to reach out and touch them. I got so I hated the sight of children. When he wanted to go visit relatives with children, I always found an excuse. It got so we stayed by ourselves more and more.

"Oh, I tried to make up for it. I tried every way I knew to please him. I spent all my time doing the things he wanted, except where children were a part of it. I cooked his favorite meals, I took trips with him, we went to plays and we read books together. But things were never the same. I guess I was trying too hard, and he wasn't trying enough. It was like he was disappointed way inside where nobody could reach it. You see, that's what I mean; I did something to him. I hurt him where it would never heal. Life never seemed to mean so much to him after that. And that operation? It wasn't serious. He shouldn't have died from that. But he did. See what I mean? I think he wanted to die because life wasn't worth living any more. I sit here and think about that, and I think I am being punished. It wasn't really my fault, and yet it was. How do you live with something like this? I wish I knew. I sit here and watch people and children, and I can't understand anything."

In a few minutes a lifetime of disappointment, guilt and remorse had been poured out. Along with it was despair and a feeling of loneliness in the face of the death that made it impossible to go back, to try to repair the damage even in words. Here was a task of trying to sort out the feelings so that the various types of guilt could be approached realistically. There was real guilt that could be met by restitution in life but not in death. There was neurotic guilt that could be brought into sharper relationship to reality. And there was existential guilt that could be met only by an awareness of the grace of God. I was trying to prepare a response that took into account the various things that had been said in the long discourse when Mrs. Lawrence started again.

"You said George talked to you about death and dying. He knew if he died I would be the one to suffer. You see, he blamed me, and nobody knows whose fault it was. He didn't say much; he was always thinking. Now I know what he was thinking." And with these words she burst into a flood of tears and wept disconsolately for a long time.

I did not try to interrupt her weeping, for I felt that she was crying for herself and for George and for the fateful events of life that had engulfed her. After her crying subsided, she said, "I am really ashamed of myself. I haven't cried like that for years."

While she had been engaged in weeping I had thought over the things she had said. Perhaps her chronic guilt about her childless state and her rejection of parenthood by adoption had produced a distorted state of mind which made her so suspicious that she began to think her husband had deliberately died to punish her, and that I was keeping secrets from her about her husband's plans for death. I had been perplexed by the nature of her responses and uncertain of the depth of her emotional maladaptation. While I was trying to determine how to be useful in resolving her state of emotional distress, something happened that changed the whole course of the interview.

She said, "But you know crying like that kind of broke something loose inside of me. When George died, I guess I was so shocked I didn't really feel much. And then when I began to think about it without all those people around, I felt angry and punished, more than I felt sad. This must sound strange to you and it does to me, too, but my feelings were every which way and none of them made sense. But crying like that seemed to do something to my feelings."

"I am glad you felt comfortable enough with me to pour out your feelings like that. You said that crying did something to your feelings. What did you mean by that?" I queried.

"I don't know, really. But I guess it was just a matter of living for twenty-five years in my own private little hell. I never breathed a word of how I felt to anyone. I was so miserable that I couldn't stand it, and yet I had to stand it because there wasn't anything else to do. But now, after all these years, I have poured it all out. It just does something to your insides. I don't think I said that very well, but I hope you understand what I mean."

Often the circumstances for self-disclosure and self-awareness are not easily defined or created. If the mood can be maintained, much psychological movement can take place in a short time. It seemed to me that this was one of those times, and I did not want to say or do anything that would disrupt it. On the other hand, I wanted to make it possible for insights to accrue. So I said, "Yes, I think you have stated it well. It is not easy to talk about things like that. But several times you spoke of things happening in your insides. Most of the important things of life happen there. Jesus spoke of the Kingdom of God as being inside a person. What did you mean specifically about the things happening inside you?"

She looked at me, and I did not know whether she felt I was prying too deeply, or whether she was trying to find out for herself what she meant before answering. She thought a while and then said, "If I told you some of the things I have thought in these quiet years, you wouldn't believe me. You have seen me in church and at meetings, and I can bet you thought I was a stable, well-adjusted person with a strong faith and few problems. But how wrong you were. I just never seemed to be comfortable with myself or anyone else, really. I was always imagining things. But I kept these things to myself. I guess I felt that if people really knew what I was like they wouldn't like me. I wanted people to like me, so I was always trying to do nice things for them. Well, that's how I was. I did nice things for people to make them like me because I didn't like myself. I didn't enjoy it. It was sort of like punishing myself so I would be fit to be with. I got tired of it, but I couldn't stop. I just kept getting more miserable. But if you looked at me, you wouldn't have known it. I guess I put on a good act."

She paused and looked out the window. I tried to respond to her feelings so that she would know I was sympathetic toward her. I said, "I think I can understand how that would be. You said over and over that you felt miserable. What do you mean by that?"

Her immediate response was, "When you are miserable, you're just plain miserable, that's all . . . I guess its mainly because I wasn't what I wanted to be. I couldn't seem to do anything about it. I was always saying and doing things I was ashamed of, but that didn't stop me from doing them. I don't know why either. Some things I couldn't control. But all the same I blamed myself. That is what made me miserable most of all. It was myself, not being what I wanted to be, that made me miserable."

"Yes, we can be deeply troubled by the things that go on inside us," I said. "But we can also draw on inner resources to resolve these troubles. Perhaps that is why you felt relieved after talking to me about those long, silent years of pent-up feeling. Some new inner resource was set free, and you feel differently about things."

"That certainly is true. I do feel much better and I can't understand why. I almost feel as if I had been forgiven. I am so glad you came to see me. You have given me lots to think about. I do hope you will come again. I guess it is really good to talk over things like these. I only wish George and I had been able to do it. Things might have been so different."

☼ ☼ ☼ ☼ ☼

This interview, using the privilege of the pastoral call, points out several things that are unique about the relationship of a pastor with his people.

In the first place, he is different whether he is willing to admit it or not. The fact that he visits in homes and hospitals and conducts funerals gives him a closeness to people that leads to trust and expressions of confidence. The pastor was the first person in twenty-five years that Mrs. Lawrence had felt able to talk with openly.

Also, the circumstances surrounding the pastor's contact with people are significant. He meets people at a time of rapid movement of the emotions, and just being there at the right time is more important than anything that is said or done. Actually, in this interview, the pastor's part was minimal, but the response was considerable. In fact, the pastor almost got in his own way a couple of times by trying to say too much. There is much to be said for the old adage, "When in doubt, listen." Paying persons the compliment of listening with concern is an act of mediating grace. Mrs. Lawrence said that she felt as if she had been forgiven, yet nothing had been said about sin or forgiveness by the pastor. The burden of her comments was the expression of failure, guilt, and remorse. No easy reassurance was given, but acceptance served as a form of grace that was recognized and responded to.

A Pastoral Call Following Death

This call illustrates something that should be kept in mind in pastoral work. Some people will not go to the pastor. As Mrs. Lawrence put it, she was not the kind that runs to doctors or pastors with her problems. But people have problems nevertheless. The added concern shown in the call is often all that is needed to begin significant communication. It is well to remember that Jesus reached people in many ways, through going to them, having them come to Him, and even having them brought to Him. But His concern was always the same, to help them find the Grace of God mediated through their relationship with Him.

ON HELPING ANOTHER MOURN

ROBERT B. REEVES, JR.

The more I try to help people who have just lost someone—and in a hospital chaplaincy, this occurs daily—the more convinced I am that the less said at such times the better. The less, that is, of religious preachment or reassurance. Of all the things inappropriate to talk about in the initial period of grief, the most inappropriate is "the will of God," let alone His love. Later on, perhaps, when the worst of the grief has been spent, such talk may bring some consolation, but not when the blow has just fallen. And frequently, when an elderly person has at last found release from prolonged pain and misery or when someone who has lived on past his proper years and has long been ready to go, finally dies, one can honestly say, "Thank God." But for the greater part, death at first brings only hurt, anger, or despair, and no kindly feelings toward the Lord.

I cringe when I hear the sentiments so many well-meaning friends and clergymen impose upon the bereaved. "It is all for the best," they may say, or "It is the will of God," or "You should not grieve, your child is with the Lord now," or "Your husband is not really gone, he has just passed over on the other side." These things may be true, but in the early stages of bereavement they are likely to appear as a mockery. If they are effective at all, it is only in squelching the expression of feelings that the consoler may find too oppressive to deal with. He protects himself, instead of comforting the bereaved.

The most valuable asset to a grieving person is to have someone who will let him grieve, who will sit quietly with him, and listen as he pours out the bitterest of his feelings, including the most hateful things about God, without feeling compelled to rise to the defense of His name. Too many people, including many clergymen, find this intolerable, for it threatens them at a point where, if they were honest, they would have to confess they have no answers. And so they try to talk the bereaved one out of his feelings, to smother his emotions and tears with platitudes of piety. When grief is suppressed this way, it is not dispelled; it is turned inward, to work havoc that may last for years, even a lifetime.

187

Perhaps the only way to help someone in the first days of grief is just to listen to him, to accept and attempt to understand his feelings until quietness returns. Then, and only then, is it appropriate to try to help him assimilate his loss into his world of meanings, and to begin to explore with him how death fits into God's scheme of things. Even then it is too soon to start providing answers, unless he seems to want them. But he must be given a lot of room for doubts and relapses into grief. The last thing to urge upon him is a platitude such as, "You must have faith." He must be allowed to *find* his faith again, and he will do so only if those who minister to him have faith enough in him to honor his grieving doubt.

In the passing of the funeral wake, we have lost one of the great sources of spiritual health. With its socialized patterns for visible and voluble mourning, the wake provided an invaluable outlet for the drama of grief, in which the immediate family were surrounded and supported by the sympathetic mourning of their friends and neighbors. After three full days, the family was ready for the funeral service and burial. The burial was stark, without any of the sentimental trimmings in which we try to conceal its meaning today. It was followed by a boisterous round of food and drink. The next day, back to work. What remained of pain and doubt was endurable, and could be worked through in the months ahead, without the terrible stress of repression that our more "civilized" customs impose.

If a person's religious faith is meaningful to him, it should help him to be honest about his feelings. It is no mark of faith to stifle grief. The deepest faith is that which permits a person to fling his bitterest accusations against God, without reproach, in the certainty that even this He understands.

IN THE EVENT OF YOUR OWN DEATH

GORDON K. BLUNT

Individuals who have to make arrangements when a close relative dies are often in an emotional state least appropriate for the conduct of any business. One of the kindest things you can do for those who are closest to you is to make a written statement of information that would be immediately useful to them in the event of death.

The following form has been prepared to assist you. You may give a copy to two or three of your closest relatives. Your pastor would also be happy to keep a copy in a permanent file at the church, where it would be immediately available. Most of the information on this form is obvious in its usefulness. If you prefer, you may attach an extra sheet giving information. Or, you may prefer simply to write your own statement, using this form merely as a guide.

In any event, we remind you also of the following information which, if it applies, ought to be immediately accessible at the time of death: Location of safe deposit boxes, tax papers, loans and debts, bank accounts and bank books, insurance policies (life, health, automobile, property), securities, bonds, savings, real estate, business interests.

A copy of the form follows:

Full name .... Soc. Sec. No. ....

Address .... Phone ....

Date of birth .... Birthplace ....

Single .... Married .... Divorced .... Widowed ....

Spouse's full name .... Marriage Date ....

Occupation .... How long? ....

Resident in this city ...... yrs. In this State ...... yrs. In U.S.A. ...... yrs.

IF A VETERAN, name of war and rank ....

    Service serial no. .... VA claim no. ....

    Date and place of entry into service ....

    Date and place of discharge ....

Father's name .... Birthplace ....

    Mother's maiden name .... Birthplace ....

Next of kin other than spouse ....

Address .... Relation ....

In emergency or death, please notify the following:

Name	Address	Relation
1.		
2.		
3.		
4.		

My attorney: .... Address ....

Location of my will: ....

Executor of my will: .... Address ....

Location of insurance policies and other valuable papers: ....

....

Other information ....

....

....

Mortuary preference, if any ....

If you wish friends to give gifts to a memorial fund rather than sending
flowers indicate to whom the gifts should be given ....

....

190

In the Event of Your Own Death

There are several alternatives with respect to what is to be done with your body after death, and there is a rather wide range of prices for an ordinary funeral. If you should give your body to a medical school and it were accepted, expenses would be nominal. If you wish your body to be taken directly to the crematory to be cremated, with a memorial service afterwards, the cost can be held to about $250. Ordinary funerals range from about $350 up; burial plots and burial costs probably vary considerably within the state.

Do you wish to contribute your body to a medical school, if possible? ....

Do you wish the minimum provision (immediate cremation), with a memorial service afterwards? ....

Do you wish a funeral with your body present in the church? ....

Name and address of church ....

If so, what is your desire about the cost? ....

....

Cemetery preference, if any ....

Do you wish your body cremated after the funeral? ....

Do you wish your body to be available to be seen by relatives and friends at the mortuary? .... In the church before the service? ....

Are there any specific hymns or music that you desire? ....

....

Other instructions and comments: ....

....

....

Witness   Signature

Witness   Date

HOPE SPRINGS ETERNAL

JAMES H. ROBINSON

Hope is the sustaining anchor of man against all despair, all defeat, and all disaster. If it did not spring eternal in the human breast, there would be no incentive to plan for the future, no inspiration to help overcome frustration. In the fulfillment of their destinies, men may be overcome and imprisoned by adversity. But, no matter whether they become prisoners of disease, environmental circumstances, ignorance, captives of a foreign enemy, or the prey of grief, so long as they continue to hope, as the Israelites did during the Babylonian captivity, they will one day break their bonds and walk free. Hope gives relief from pessimism and fosters in the heart and mind an optimism which inspires us to transcend our misfortunes.

We look for some counterpart of the Kingdom of Heaven to appear on earth. No matter how long it is delayed, we continue to lay hold with impatient hands upon every means that we can use to achieve it. In St. Paul's epistle on love, and in his hymn on love, I Corinthians 13:13, he ends by saying, "And now abideth faith, hope, charity." This hope springs from God, and Divine hope is a firm expectation of all promised good things, so far as they may be according to His will.

Divine hope is distinguished from carnal presumptions by its inseparable effect, for it has a cleansing efficacy: as the writer of John 3:3 declares, "Every man who hath this hope in him, purifieth himself, even as he is pure."

The poet, stricken by his personal grief, survives because he is sustained by hope. The immortal elegy *In Memoriam* was written by Alfred Lord Tennyson upon the death of his closest friend, Arthur Henry Hallam. The poet was in deep despair, but he wrote in the hope that he would be sustained by his faith in God. A memorable line from this poem speaks of the "mighty hopes that make us men." Hope is a force essential to life.

And Oliver Goldsmith's lines from his poem *The Captivity* speak with great relevance:

Hope, like the taper's gleaming light,
Adorns the wretch's way;
And still, as darker grows the night,
Emits a brighter ray.

REMARRIAGE

JOSEPH C. LANDRUD

Writing in *But Not to Lose*,* Landrud states:

"As we experience release from paralyzing guilt, it is natural that we return to life with a steadily increasing eagerness and zest. We emerge from the cold deep well of self-confinement into the warming sun of revitalizing personal relationships. Before we know it, we may even find ourselves in love again. This is both wonderful and frightening. It is wonderful because it is unexpected, unplanned, yet we have the happy realization that the void in our lives is filled with new love. But it is frightening to acknowledge that it has actually happened, frightening to admit to ourselves that we are in love again.

"Such a new love may seem to minimize or even cheapen the love we felt for our now-deceased love. True, by this time we are freed of the guilt in connection with that earlier death. But now, by virtue of our new love, we may begin to feel guilty about not feeling guilty.

"The way out of this seeming impasse is to return in meditation to the *quality* of our love relationship with the departed. Was that love relationship truly free, spontaneous, self-giving and life-affirming? If so, it is without end and non-limiting. This is, it is no healthy testimony to the quality of our love for someone to say that when he or she died our ability to love also died. Authentic love which, in its deepest form is the love of God expressed through us to all, without limit and without end, could certainly find a new object in the world around us. It is this deep and limitless love that truly makes us free."

---

* Austin H. Kutscher (Editor), *But Not to Lose*, New York, Frederick Fell, Inc., 1969.

F. APPROACHES BY THE MINISTRY TO RECOVERY FROM BEREAVEMENT

RESULTS OF A SURVEY:
OPINIONS OF CLERGY, WIDOWS AND WIDOWERS

AUSTIN H. KUTSCHER and AUSTIN H. KUTSCHER, JR.

One of the major areas of this book, that for which the assistance of professional consultants and widows or widowers was sought, is concerned with the results of a multiple-choice type of survey from which was derived a vital and definitive consensus of information on the general subject of desirable, practical approaches to recovery from grief. Thus, the multiple-choice opinionnaire completed by these two groups of experienced people dealt with the advice they believed *ought* to be given to individuals with regard to certain of the specific practicalities or problems with which one has to deal as a bereaved person.

Those qualified to speak, we believed, were among practitioners of internal medicine, general surgeons, and general practitioners of medicine; among physician-analysts and psychiatrists; clergymen, rabbis, and professional counselors; as well as among specialists who devote themselves to paramedical or other endeavors. All in all the responses of forty clergymen, randomly selected from Western faiths, were included in the survey tabulation.

From consultants it was hoped that a balance of informed opinions would become available to serve as guidelines for those who wished advice on a very considerable number of bothersome problems—problems very real to the bereaved but to which our more formal contributors had not chosen to address themselves.

The presentation of the consensus opinion is thus based on the simple concept that if, in truth, there is such a thing as working one's way through grief and mourning, clergymen, among others, may well have important suggestions as to better ways to accomplish this as well as some ways which may be worse or even detrimental to the process and the individual's progress. To the suggestions of the clergymen, in this presentation have been added the opinions of widows and widowers, members of Parents Without Partners, whose advice was considered distinctly pertinent.

The questionnaire covered six categories:

(I) Signs and symptoms of bereavement

(II) Guilt and bereavement

(III) What the bereaved should be told by the physician

(IV) What the bereaved should be encouraged to do

(V) Advice concerning remarriage

If the opinions concur with the bereaved's own inclinations, they should serve as a source of *comfort, satisfaction* and *encouragement.* If the bereaved had no opinion in a particular regard, adopting these consultants' advice would ordinarily be a wise course of action. However, if the reader finds himself in disagreement, it might be well for him to review the circumstances which might have contributed to these divergent feelings. Likewise, it might be desirable for him to consider shifting his course of action to one more in the direction suggested by the consultants. Where divergences between consultant opinions and those of the bereaved are encountered, they are best looked on principally as matters upon which the individual might well dwell longer—perhaps to explore his feelings further and perhaps to seek additional advice. In any event, through such further consideration, hopefully, the bereaved should be either more fully secure in his *own* divergent course of action or more amenable to change.

In the final sense, it is hoped that the consultant opinion will help the bereaved-to-be or the bereaved to further find himself as a loving, believing individual at peace with himself, his society, and his God.

I. Signs and Symptoms of Bereavement

1. In the case of a prolonged illness with a probably fatal outcome, do you believe that bereavement and grief (for the "bereaved-to-be") make an appearance prior to the death of the individual?

	Always	Frequently	Sometimes	Rarely	Never	No Answer
All Clergy	12.2	51.2	26.8	7.3	0.0	2.4
Total W/W	16.0	32.0	28.0	7.2	9.6	7.2

Results of a Survey: Opinions of Clergy, Widows and Widowers

2a. Are the following occurrences to be expected by the bereaved: Dreams of the deceased?

	Always	Frequently	Sometimes	Rarely	Never	No Answer
All Clergy	2.4	56.1	34.1	2.4	0.0	4.9
Total W/W	10.4	28.8	48	7.2	3.2	2.4

2b. Illusions of the presence of the deceased?

	Always	Frequently	Sometimes	Rarely	Never	No Answer
All Clergy	0.0	31.7	46.3	17.1	2.4	2.4
Total W/W	2.4	9.6	39.2	24.8	21.6	2.4

2c. Angry thoughts concerning the deceased?

	Always	Frequently	Sometimes	Rarely	Never	No Answer
All Clergy	0.0	14.6	53.7	24.4	2.4	4.9
Total W/W	0.8	8.0	33.6	28.0	24.8	4.8

2d. Guilt feelings towards the deceased?

	Always	Frequently	Sometimes	Rarely	Never	No Answer
All Clergy	2.4	56.1	31.7	4.9	2.4	2.4
Total W/W	3.2	16.0	37.6	16.8	21.6	4.8

2e. Feelings of infidelity in relation to the deceased?

	Always	Frequently	Sometimes	Rarely	Never	No Answer
All Clergy	0.0	14.6	63.4	12.2	4.9	4.9
Total W/W	0.0	4.0	24.0	29.6	37.6	4.8

2f. Feelings of despair, emptiness, and hopelessness?

	Always	Frequently	Sometimes	Rarely	Never	No Answer
All Clergy	17.1	56.1	22.0	0.0	2.4	2.4
Total W/W	27.2	30.4	23.2	3.2	13.6	2.4

2g. Feelings of helplessness?

	Always	Frequently	Sometimes	Rarely	Never	No Answer
All Clergy	9.8	58.5	26.8	2.4	0.0	2.4
Total W/W	16.0	22.4	42.4	12.8	3.2	3.2

2h. Loss of appetite and/or weight loss?

	Always	Frequently	Sometimes	Rarely	Never	No Answer
All Clergy	0.0	34.1	58.5	4.9	0.0	2.4
Total W/W	12	28.8	40.8	14.4	2.4	1.6

2i. Sleeplessness?

	Always	Frequently	Sometimes	Rarely	Never	No Answer
All Clergy	7.3	51.2	36.6	2.4	0.0	2.4
Total W/W	19.2	35.2	33.6	8.8	3.2	0

2j. Appearance of subjective symptoms similar to those of the deceased?

	Always	Frequently	Sometimes	Rarely	Never	No Answer
All Clergy	0.0	12.2	56.1	22.0	2.4	7.3
Total W/W	0.8	5.6	21.6	26.4	40.8	4.8

2k. Impotence?

	Always	Frequently	Sometimes	Rarely	Never	No Answer
All Clergy	0.0	14.6	43.9	26.8	2.4	12.2
Total W/W	3.2	7.2	21.6	24.0	25.6	18.4

2l. Diminished sexual desire?

	Always	Frequently	Sometimes	Rarely	Never	No Answer
All Clergy	0.0	22.0	48.8	19.5	2.4	7.3
Total W/W	10.4	14.4	33.5	17.6	20.8	3.2

2m. Inclination towards the practice of masturbation?

	Always	Frequently	Sometimes	Rarely	Never	No Answer
All Clergy	0.0	7.3	65.9	12.2	2.4	12.2
Total W/W	2.4	6.4	31.2	24.8	31.2	4.0

II. Guilt and Bereavement

3. Is guilt less likely when there has been free expression of feelings between the dying person and the "bereaved-to-be"?

	Always	Frequently	Sometimes	Rarely	Never	No Answer
All Clergy	41.5	48.8	9.8	0.0	0.0	0.0
Total W/W	42.4	27.2	15.2	7.2	1.6	6.4

Results of a Survey: Opinions of Clergy, Widows and Widowers

4a. Are guilt experiences to be expected by the bereaved when he/she: Puts away pictures of the deceased?

	Always	Frequently	Sometimes	Rarely	Never	No Answer
All Clergy	2.4	34.1	41.5	12.2	2.4	7.3
Total W/W	5.6	12.0	28.8	27.2	24.8	1.6

4b. Begins to function on his or her own?

	Always	Frequently	Sometimes	Rarely	Never	No Answer
All Clergy	0.0	19.5	34.1	34.1	4.9	7.3
Total W/W	4.0	11.2	22.4	20.8	38.4	3.2

4c. Begins to find pleasure once again?

	Always	Frequently	Sometimes	Rarely	Never	No Answer
All Clergy	0.0	14.6	56.1	19.5	2.4	7.3
Total W/W	4.8	10.4	28.8	24.0	29.6	2.4

4d. Accepts the inevitability of the deceased's death?

	Always	Frequently	Sometimes	Rarely	Never	No Answer
All Clergy	0.0	14.6	34.1	41.5	2.4	7.3
Total W/W	4.8	7.2	28.8	20.0	36.8	2.4

4e. Begins to take up old or new interests again?

	Always	Frequently	Sometimes	Rarely	Never	No Answer
All Clergy	0.0	12.2	43.9	34.1	2.4	7.3
Total W/W	3.2	4.8	28.8	26.4	34.4	2.4

4f. Begins to have renewed interest in members of the opposite sex?

	Always	Frequently	Sometimes	Rarely	Never	No Answer
All Clergy	0.0	39.0	41.5	9.8	2.4	7.3
Total W/W	7.2	13.6	29.6	20.0	27.2	2.4

4g. Decides to remarry?

	Always	Frequently	Sometimes	Rarely	Never	No Answer
All Clergy	4.9	31.7	36.6	17.1	2.4	7.3
Total W/W	12.0	12.8	17.6	19.2	36.0	2.4

5. When is it normal for the bereaved spouse to begin to experience some pleasure again? (Check one)

   Code

   (a) A few days after the funeral
   (b) A week or so after the funeral
   (c) A few weeks after the deceased passed away
   (d) A month or two or three after the deceased passed away
   (e) Six months after the deceased passed away
   (f) Later only

	a	b	c	d	e	f	No Answer
Total W/W	2.4	3.2	13.6	36.0	35.2	0	9.6
All Clergy	22.0	14.6	17.1	24.4	7.3	7.3	7.3

III. What the Bereaved Should Be Told by the Physician

6. Is it important that the bereaved be advised how often death is faced by the dying with serenity?

	Always	Frequently	Sometimes	Rarely	Never	No Answer
All Clergy	24.4	41.5	29.3	4.9	0.0	0.0
Total W/W	22.4	18.4	36.8	9.6	8.8	4.0

7. Should the "bereaved-to-be" be made aware of the patient's right to die without prolonged but futile efforts?

	Always	Frequently	Sometimes	Rarely	Never	No Answer
All Clergy	34.1	36.6	22.0	4.9	2.4	0.0
Total W/W	40.8	11.2	24.8	4.0	12.0	7.2

8. Should the physician advise the bereaved in detail that everything was done?

	Always	Frequently	Sometimes	Rarely	Never	No Answer
All Clergy	34.1	39.0	24.4	2.4	0.0	0.0
Total W/W	58.4	8.0	17.6	8.8	4.8	2.4

9. Should emphasis in comforting the bereaved be placed on the fact that he has "no place to go but up?"

	Always	Frequently	Sometimes	Rarely	Never	No Answer
All Clergy	7.3	7.3	22.0	31.7	26.8	4.9
Total W/W	12.8	12.8	26.4	17.6	26.4	4.0

10. Should the bereaved be encouraged to appreciate that following his great loss, he may well experience lessened fear of future sorrow, tragedy, and death?

	Always	Frequently	Sometimes	Rarely	Never	No Answer
All Clergy	9.8	17.1	39.0	26.8	0.0	7.3
Total W/W	9.6	12.8	29.6	12.8	31.2	4.0

11. Should emphasis be placed upon the fact that fortunately the bereaved has a child (or children) by the departed spouse?

	Always	Frequently	Sometimes	Rarely	Never	No Answer
All Clergy	14.6	29.3	41.5	7.3	0.0	7.3
Total W/W	28.0	12.8	37.6	16.0	4.0	1.6

12. With regard to the autopsy permission, do you believe that (Check one or more):

The bereaved should be strongly urged to give his consent 44.

The bereaved should be encouraged to give his consent 45.

No pressure should be put on the bereaved to give his consent 46.

If the bereaved is reluctant to give his consent, he should be encouraged to ascertain how truly important and significant the autopsy findings might be to the doctors involved and to act accordingly 47.

	44	45	46	47	No Answer
All Clergy	6.3	36.5	15.9	41.3	0.0
Total W/W	8.9	21.3	24.9	45.0	0

IV. What the Bereaved Should Be Encouraged to Do

13. Would psychiatric advice be desirable for the "bereaved-to-be"?

	Always	Frequently	Sometimes	Rarely	Never	No Answer
All Clergy	2.4	7.3	53.7	24.1	0.0	2.4
Total W/W	5.6	11.2	57.6	15.2	4.8	5.6

14. Would regular visits to a physician during and for the first year of bereavement be desirable?

	Always	Frequently	Sometimes	Rarely	Never	No Answer
All Clergy	2.4	9.8	63.4	22.0	2.4	0.0
Total W/W	13.6	15.2	43.2	20.0	4.8	3.2

15. Ought a bereaved individual be hospitalized for an elective procedure soon after or during the course of bereavement?

	Yes	Pref. Not	Never	No Answer
All Clergy	4.9	80.5	7.3	7.3
Total W/W	4.8	69.6	20.	5.6

16. Should crying be encouraged?

	Always	Frequently	Sometimes	Rarely	Never	No Answer
All Clergy	24.4	36.6	36.6	0.0	0.0	2.4
Total W/W	24.8	19.2	44.0	5.6	2.4	4.0

17. Should repression of distressing memories (such as the time of and sight of death) be encouraged and supported?

	Always	Frequently	Sometimes	Rarely	Never	No Answer
All Clergy	12.2	12.2	17.1	41.5	14.6	2.4
Total W/W	7.2	9.6	32.0	20.8	24.8	5.6

18. Should the bereaved be encouraged to discuss suicidal thoughts and feelings?

	Always	Frequently	Sometimes	Rarely	Never	No Answer
All Clergy	29.3	19.5	31.7	7.3	7.3	4.9
Total W/W	29.6	7.2	28.8	4.8	22.4	7.2

19a. Should he/she be encouraged to talk about a recent bereavement with: Old friends?

	Always	Frequently	Sometimes	Rarely	Never	No Answer
All Clergy	24.4	39.0	31.7	4.9	0.0	0.0
Total W/W	21.6	20	45.6	6.4	1.6	4.8

19b. New friends?

	Always	Frequently	Sometimes	Rarely	Never	No Answer
All Clergy	0.0	12.2	56.1	26.8	2.4	2.4
Total W/W	0.8	3.2	36.0	40.	9.6	10.4

19c. Someone who has had a similar experience?

	Always	Frequently	Sometimes	Rarely	Never	No Answer
All Clergy	26.8	29.3	43.9	0.0	0.0	0.0
Total W/W	26.4	24.0	41.6	3.2	0.8	4.0

20. With regard to the bereaved's feelings relating to the deceased, should he be encouraged to express these to: (Check one or more)

	A Friend	A relative	A clergyman	Others	No One	No Answer
All Clergy	33.0	24.5	35.5	6.4	0.0	0.0
Total W/W	30.5	23.9	29.7	8.1	4.2	3.5

21. What do you feel is best done with the deceased's wedding ring and when?

	Keep permanently	Keep a while	Discard	No Answer	Other	Give to member of family
All Clergy	56.1	17.1	0.0	2.4	29.3	
Total W/W	50.8	4.0	3.2	4.0	27.8	10.3

22. Should the bereaved be encouraged to: (Check one or more)

Code

(a) Keep some of the deceased's personal belongings?

(b) Destroy the deceased's belongings?

(c) Put the personal belongings of the deceased in storage— available but out of sight?

(d) Leave the deceased's personal belongings undisturbed?

(e) Give some of the deceased's personal belongings away to family and friends?

(f) Give some of the deceased's belongings away to a charity?

	a	b	c	d	e	f	No Answer
All Clergy	24.0	1.0	1.0	1.0	33.3	37.5	2.0
Total W/W	23.4	3.2	6.5	1.4	29.1	35.6	0.7

23. Ought the bereaved, if religiously inclined, be encouraged to go to religious services on the days which have a special significance with regard to the deceased?

	Always	Frequently	Sometimes	Rarely	Never	No Answer
All Clergy	22.0	34.1	29.3	4.9	0.0	9.8
Total W/W	24.0	22.4	32.8	10.4	8.8	1.6

207

24a. Should the person in grief be encouraged to: Obtain a dog or a pet?

	Always	Frequently	Sometimes	Rarely	Never	No Answer
All Clergy	0.0	9.8	58.5	17.1	2.4	12.2
Total W/W	0.8	12.8	55.2	10.4	12.0	8.8

24b. Seek a companion (if elderly)?

	Always	Frequently	Sometimes	Rarely	Never	No Answer
All Clergy	2.4	36.6	43.9	4.9	0.0	12.2
Total W/W	7.2	29.6	42.4	7.2	4.8	8.8

24c. Travel?

	Always	Frequently	Sometimes	Rarely	Never	No Answer
All Clergy	9.8	22.0	51.2	2.4	0.0	14.6
Total W/W	6.3	23.6	57.5	4.7	1.6	6.8

24d. Go shopping?

	Always	Frequently	Sometimes	Rarely	Never	No Answer
All Clergy	9.8	26.8	48.8	2.4	0.0	12.2
Total W/W	11.2	28.0	46.4	6.4	3.2	4.8

24e. Change jobs if he had long wanted to do so?

	Always	Frequently	Sometimes	Rarely	Never	No Answer
All Clergy	14.6	39.0	24.4	9.8	0.0	12.2
Total W/W	19.2	22.4	36.0	12.0	2.4	8.0

24f. Move to a new living location?

	Always	Frequently	Sometimes	Rarely	Never	No Answer
All Clergy	0.0	4.9	56.1	24.4	0.0	14.6
Total W/W	0	11.2	40.0	25.6	17.6	5.6

24g. Seek vocational guidance (discuss problems at work, job aptitude) at this time?

	Always	Frequently	Sometimes	Rarely	Never	No Answer
All Clergy	2.4	12.2	56.1	9.8	2.4	17.1
Total W/W	13.6	12.0	39.2	17.6	8.0	9.6

25. Is working good for the bereaved?

	Always	Frequently	Sometimes	Rarely	Never	No Answer
All Clergy	41.5	48.8	7.3	0.0	0.0	2.4
Total W/W	63.2	28.0	6.4	0	0	2.4

26. When do you believe the bereaved should be encouraged to resume work?

	Almost Immediately	Within a Week	Within 2 Weeks	Only When He Feels "up to it"	No Answer
All Clergy	26.8	36.6	22.0	12.2	2.4
Total W/W	30.2	20.6	31.7	13.5	4.0

27. Should the bereaved make major decisions as early as possible?

	Always	Frequently	Sometimes	Rarely	Never	No Answer
All Clergy	9.8	17.1	24.4	39.0	7.3	2.4
Total W/W	22.4	14.4	17.6	21.6	20.0	4.0

28. To whom do you believe the bereaved should turn for advice? (Check one or more)

> *Code*
>
> (a) Clergy
>
> (b) Physician
>
> (c) Psychiatrist
>
> (d) Lawyer
>
> (e) Psychologist
>
> (f) Reading

	a	b	c	d	e	f	No Answer
Total W/W	27.2	20.8	7.7	25.2	6.4	10.2	2.6

29. To what extent do you believe a bereaved should seek advice? (Check one or more)

	A Great Deal	Considerable	Minimal	None	No Answer
All Clergy					
Total W/W	7.0	28.7	53.5	1.6	9.3

30. When should the bereaved begin to seek advice? (Check one)

  Code

  (a) At once

  (b) During the first few days

  (c) Soon after the funeral

  (d) After a week or two

  (e) Later

	a	b	c	d	e	No Answer
Total W/W	11.4	9.8	21.2	25.0	21.2	10.6

31. How should the bereaved deal with promises of a general nature made to the deceased during life? (Check one or more)

  Code

  (a) Follow them, if practical and reasonable

  (b) Follow them, even if not practical

  (c) Disregard them, if the bereaved so wishes, even if practical and reasonable

  (e) Disregard all

	a	b	c	d	e	No Answer
Total W/W	73.2	0	6.0	17.4	1.3	2.0

32. Should the bereaved: (Check one)

	Begin new hobbies	Continue old hobbies	Both	No Answer
All Clergy	4.9	29.3	58.5	7.3
Total W/W	7.2	3.2	88.0	1.6

33. Should the bereaved be encouraged to relinquish excessive attachments to the deceased?

	Always	Frequently	Sometimes	Rarely	Never	No Answer
All Clergy	46.3	34.1	9.8	7.3	0.0	2.4
Total W/W	52.8	19.2	17.6	2.4	5.6	2.4

V. Advice Concerning Remarriage

34. Should the bereaved be encouraged to remarry if age permits?

	Yes	No	No Answer
All Clergy	82.9	4.9	12.2
Total W/W	92.0	4.8	3.2

35. Is remarriage the major long range problem to be dealt with by a relatively young bereaved spouse?

	Yes	No	No Answer
All Clergy	56.1	26.8	17.1
Total W/W	78.4	18.4	3.2

36. Should the bereaved be encouraged to believe that he has much to offer in a new marital relationship despite previous involvement and loss?

	Always	Frequently	Sometimes	Rarely	Never	No Answer
All Clergy	41.5	41.5	4.9	2.4	0.0	9.8
Total W/W	58.2	23.2	14.4	0	0.8	3.2

37. Is it true that, following the death of a spouse, those who have loved deeply and satisfyingly tend to move more quickly to remarry when compared with those who have been embittered by marriage?

	Yes	No	No Answer
All Clergy	56.1	22.0	22.0
Total W/W	59.2	36.8	4.0

38. Should the bereaved be encouraged towards remarriage for the sake of any young children?

	Always	Frequently	Sometimes	Rarely	Never	No Answer
All Clergy	4.9	31.7	41.5	14.0	2.4	4.9
Total W/W	7.2	18.4	36.0	15.2	19.2	4.0

39. Would remarriage for a widow or widower be best with another widow or widower?

	Always	Frequently	Sometimes	Rarely	Never	No Answer
All Clergy	2.4	36.6	51.2	0.0	0.0	9.8
Total W/W	8.8	42.4	40.8	4.0	0	4.0

211

40. Is it desirable to encourage the bereaved to make the decision as to whether or not he or she will remarry *before* a particular person is considered?

	Yes	No	No Answer
All Clergy	46.3	46.3	7.3
Total W/W	40.4	63.2	6.4

41. Is it desirable to inform relatives and in-laws of a decision to remarry before a specific person is considered?

	Yes	No	No Answer
All Clergy	29.3	68.3	2.4
Total W/W	16.8	80.0	3.2

G. ANTHOLOGY OF LITERATURE

SELECTED READINGS

ROBERT B. REEVES, JR.

A baby is God's opinion that life should go on.

(Carl Sandburg)

In the University of Oxford, above the entrance to the Department of Anatomy, there is the following inscription: "This is the place where death serves life."

(Sidney Greenberg)

We do not believe in immortality because we have proved it, but we forever try to prove it because we believe it.

(James Martineau)

I find the great thing in this world is not so much where we stand, as in what direction we are moving. To reach the port of heaven, we must sail sometimes with the wind, and sometimes against it; but we must sail, and not drift, nor lie at anchor.

(Oliver Wendell Holmes)

In true married love, it is not so much that two hearts walk side by side through life. Rather, the two hearts become one heart. That is why death is not the separation of two hearts, but the tearing apart of one heart. It is this that makes the bitterness of grief.

(Fulton J. Sheen)

With every rising of the sun
Think of your life as just begun.
The past is cancelled and buried deep—
All "yesterdays"—there let them sleep!

(Author unknown)

At times the dead are closer to us than the living, and the wisdom and affection of the past stretch blessing hands over our lives, projecting a guardian care out of the shadows and helping us over hard places. For there are certain kinds of love that few but the very wise fully understand until they have become memories.

(Hans Zinsser)

Strangely, these very memories which ultimately help us to cheat death are likely to be quite painful while the anguish of parting is still fresh.

(Sidney Greenberg)

He who is well lives well
He who lives well loves well
He who loves well cries well
He who cries well becomes well
He who becomes well loves again
And dies well

(Sandra Bess)

INHERITANCE

God grant you sweet music
  at each eventide,
God grant you a book
  of verse by your side,
God grant you a friendship
  glowing with laughter,
God grant you the promise
  of peace ever-after.

Go swift on your voyage
  with hope in your heart,
Take with you the love
  we each do impart.
The doubts and the fears
  He now will dispel,
His radiance beckons . . .
  beloved, farewell!

(Sandra Bess)

H. ANTHOLOGY OF MUSIC

MUSIC SELECTIONS

The following selections suggest music that is available for use at a memorial service or during the early stages of bereavement. It is not meant to be complete, and emphasizes only music by well-known composers of our Western tradition since the sixteenth century.

Since death is a wholly personal experience, the music selected for a memorial service may be in some way associated with the deceased. Perhaps a word of caution is, therefore, to be wisely interposed at this point: If the music played at the funeral is something which had an intimate meaning for the bereaved and the deceased, the psychological association may later be deleterious for the bereaved. He may never hear it again with pleasure, remembering that it accompanied the loved one on the last journey. His delight in this music for its own sake is spoiled; he cannot enjoy the feeling formerly shared when it was played; he loses the restorative influence of a happy memory, depriving himself, in the months and years to come, of the loving remembrance that can be evoked by listening to a familiar melody that has deep associations for him.

Perhaps, then, other music befitting the sad occasion of services for the departed should be selected. The list which is offered here contains not only distinctive funeral music but great religious music from innumerable sources, as well as symphonic or choral excerpts of a solemn and noble character, suitable, although not intrinsically meant for this use, on the occasion of death. Every taste can be satisfied with some choice from such a compilation of profoundly moving musics.

Amram, David	*Dirge and Variations—viola and piano
Anerto, Giovanni	*Missa Pro Defuncti—chorus
Bach, J. S.	*Christ Lay in Death's Dark Prison (Cantata No. 18)—chorus *Come, Soothing Death—chorus *Death, I Do Not Fear Thee—chorus *Come, Sweet Hour of Death— (Cantata No. 161)—chorus

---

*—recording available

	*God's Time is the Best (Cantata No. 106)—chorus *Trauer Ode (Funeral Ode)—chorus *Mass in B Minor—chorus *The Passion According to St. John—chorus *The Passion According to St. Matthew— chorus *Any of the organ Preludes and Fugues *Selections from "German Organ Mass"
Barber, Samuel	*Adagio for Strings
Barnby, Joseph	*Crossing the Bar—chorus
Beethoven, Ludwig van	*Cantata on the Death of Emperor Joseph II —chorus and orchestra Elegy—chorus *Funeral March from Symphony No. 3 (Eroica)—orchestra *Missa Solemnis—chorus and orchestra *Selections from "Mount of Olives"—chorus and orchestra
Berlioz, Hector	*Symphony Funêbre et Triomphale— orchestra *Requiem—chorus *Death scene from Romeo et Juliette— orchestra
Billings, William	*Selections from Hymns and Anthems—chorus
Bloch, Ernest	*Baal Shem—violin and piano *Selections from Sacred Service—chorus and orchestra
Blow, John	*Ode on the Death of Mr. Henry Purcell— chorus
Brahms, Johannes	*Chorale Preludes—organ *A German Requiem—chorus and orchestra *O Death—from *Four Serious Songs*— voice and piano A German Requiem—organ score *Tragic Overture—orchestra
Britten, Benjamin	*Sinfonia da Requiem—orchestra *Lachrymae—viola and piano *War Requiem—chorus and orchestra
Bruch, Max	*Kol Nidrei—cello and orchestra

Music Selections

Bruckner, Anton	*Mass No. 2—chorus and orchestra *Mass No. 3—chorus and orchestra *Psalm 150—chorus and orchestra Requiem—chorus
Buck, Dudley	Crossing the Bar—voice and piano
Byrd, William	*Mass in Three Parts—chorus
Campra, Andre	*Requiem—chorus and orchestra
Cherubini, Luigi	*Requiem in C minor—chorus and orchestra *Requiem in D minor—chorus and orchestra
Chopin, Frederic	*Marche Funèbre from Second Piano Sonata
Dowland, John	*Lachrymae—chorus and orchestra
Dubois, Theodore	*Adoremus Te, Christe (from *Seven Last Words*)—chorus
Durufle, Maurice	*Requiem—chorus and orchestra
Dvorak, Antonin	*Requiem—chorus and orchestra
Eberlin, Ernst	Grief Is in My Heart—chorus
Faure, J. B.	Crucifixus—voice and piano
Faure, Gabriel	*Elegie—cello and orchestra *Requiem—chorus and orchestra Requiem—organ score
Franck,	Panis Angelicus—chorus Cantabile—organ Chorales—organ
Gallus, Jacobus	Lo, Now Is the Death of the Just Man—chorus
Gaul, A. R.	They That Sow in Tears (from *The Holy City*)—chorus
Guilmant, Alexandre	Marche Funèbre—organ
Guion, David	Prayer—voice and piano Prayer—chorus
Gounod, Charles	The King of Love My Shepherd Is—voice and piano Messe Solennells—chorus and orchestra Requiem I Requiem II Requiem III

Grieg, Edvard	Ase's Death (from *Peer Gynt*)—orchestra Ase's Death (from *Peer Gynt*)—piano solo God's Peace Is Eternal—chorus Two Elegiac Melodies—orchestra
Handel, G. F.	Trust in the Lord (after the Largo from "Xerxes") chorus Selections from *The Messiah*—chorus
Haydn, Joseph	*Symphony No. 44 (Trauer)—orchestra *Seven Last Words of Christ—chorus and orchestra Darkness Obscured the Earth—chorus
Hindemith, Paul	*When Lilacs Last in the Dooryard Bloom'd—chorus *Requiem *For Those We Love*—chorus and orchestra *Trauermusik—viola and strings
Holst, Gustav	*Dirge for Two Veterans—chorus
Kabalevsky, Dmitri	*Requiem—chorus and orchestra
Kinder	Meditation—organ
La Forge, F.	Before the Crucifix—voice and piano Before the Crucifix—chorus
DeLassus, Orlando	*Requiem—chorus and orchestra
LaRue, Pierre de	*Requiem—chorus and orchestra
Liszt, Franz	Funeral Music for Mosonyi's Death—piano solo To the Memory of Petofi—piano solo The Funeral Gondola I—piano solo The Funeral Gondola II—piano solo Richard Wagner, Venice—piano solo
Mahler, Gustav	*The Farewell from *Das Lied von der Erde* (Songs of the Earth)—voice and orchestra *Kindertotenlieder—voice and orchestra
Malipiero, Gian Francesco	Sinfonia del Silenzio e della Morte—orchestra Missa Pro Mortuis—chorus
Malotte, A. H.	The Lord's Prayer—chorus The Lord's Prayer—voice and piano The Lord's Prayer—organ

	23rd Psalm—voice and piano 23rd Psalm—chorus
Mendelssohn, Felix	*Funeral March—orchestra If With All Your Hearts—chorus
Monteverdi, Claudio	*Lament (from *Arianna*)—chorus
Morely, Thomas	Thou Knowest, Lord—chorus
Mozart, W. A.	*Ave, verum corpus—chorus and orchestra *Masonic Funeral Music—orchestra *Requiem—chorus and orchestra
Mueller, Carl F.	Create in Me a Clean Heart—chorus
Mussorgsky, Modest	*Songs and Dances of Death—song cycle
Noble, T. T.	Souls of the Righteous—chorus
Palestrina, Giovanni	*Messa Papae Marcelli—chorus O Gentle Death—Chorus The Strife is O'er—chorus
Poulenc, Francis	*Elegie for Horn and Piano
Purcell, Henry	Now, O Lord, I Lay Me Down—chorus *Music for the Funeral of Queen Mary— chorus and orchestra *When I am Laid in Earth (from *Dido and Aeneas*)—aria
Rachmaninoff, Sergei	*Isle of the Dead—orchestra Vocalise—voice and piano
Ravel, Maurice	*Pavane Pour Une Infanta Defunte—orchestra
Rheinberger, Joseph	Vision—organ
Roberts, J. V.	Peace I Leave With You—chorus
Rodney, Paul	Calvary—voice and piano Calvary—chorus
Saint-Saens, Camille	Requiem
Salter, S.	Gethsemane—voice and piano
Schubert, Franz	*Death and the Maiden—voice and piano *Death and the Maiden—slow movement of string quartet The Lord is My Shepherd—chorus

Schuman, William	*Carols of Death—chorus
Schutz, Heinrich	*A German Requiem—chorus and orchestra
Shelley, H. R.	The King of Love My Shepherd is— voice and piano
	The King of Love My Shepherd is— chorus
Sibelius, Jean	*Swan of Tuonela—orchestra
	*Valse Triste—orchestra
Stravinsky, Igor	*Elegie—for unaccompanied violin or viola
	*In Memoriam, Dylan Thomas—chorus and orchestra
Sullivan, Arthur	God Shall Wipe Away All Tears—chorus
Tallis, Thomas	*Lamentations of Jeremiah—chorus
Vaughn Williams, R.	*Dona Nobis Pacem—chorus and orchestra
Verdi, Guiseppe	*Requiem in Memory of Manzoni—chorus and orchestra
Wagner, Richard	*Gotterdammerung: Funeral Music— orchestra
	*Trauermusik for wind instruments.
Zechiel	Entrust to Him Thy Footsteps—organ
	Any hymns from Protestant and Catholic hymnals